The Philosophy Files 2

Stephen Law on Stephen Law

'How did I arrive at philosophy? At the age of 17 I fell 65 feet head first off a cliff. Some say I never really recovered. I was thrown out of sixth form and never did get any A-Levels.

'After a number of dead-end jobs I ended up working as a postman in Cambridge for four years. While I was a postman I read a lot. One book led me to another and eventually I ended up reading nothing but philosophy books. I found that philosophy books addressed those really big questions that had always bothered me and that most other disciplines just skirt around or ignore.

'I managed to gain a place at The City University, London to study for a degree in philosophy. I got a first and that enabled me to get funding to go to Oxford University where I obtained my doctorate. I have held a number of lectureships at Oxford colleges and I'm currently a Lecturer in Philosophy at Heythrop College, University of London.

'I have lots of interest outside philosophy. I still live in Oxford where I play drums in local jazz and Latin bands. And I like to climb, especially in the Alps.'

More information about Stephen Law and philosophy can be found at www.thinking-big.co.uk

Also by Stephen Law

The Philosophy Files

The Philosophy Files 2

(previously published as *The Outer Limits*)

Stephen Law
Illustrated by Daniel Postgate

Orion
Children's Books

First published in Great Britain in 2003
as *The Outer Limits*
This paperback edition published in Great Britain in 2006
by Orion Children's Books
a division of the Orion Publishing Group Ltd
Orion House
5 Upper St Martin's Lane
London WC2H 9EA

The Orion Publishing Group's policy is to use papers that are natural, renewable
and recylable products and made from wood grown in sustainable forests.
The logging and manufacturing processes are expected to conform to the
environmental regulations of the country of origin.

A catalogue record for this book is available from the British Library
Printed in Great Britain

ISBN-10 1 84255 525 1
ISBN-13 978 1 84255 525 5

www.orionbooks.co.uk

For Freyja and Ferne, Alex and Hamish

Contents

Introduction

Chapter 1. Astrology, flying saucers and ESP 1

Chapter 2. Killing people 33

Chapter 3. Does Murderous Mick deserve
to be punished? 57

Chapter 4. Where did the universe come from? 80

Chapter 5. Is time travel possible? 115

Chapter 6. Could a machine think? 141

Chapter 7. But is it science? 167

Some Useful Words 197

Introduction

Travelling to the Outer Limits

This is a philosophy book. That means it's a book of *mysteries*: some of the deepest and most exciting mysteries of all.

Have you ever wondered where the universe came from?

Or whether it is OK to execute murderers?

Or if a machine could think?

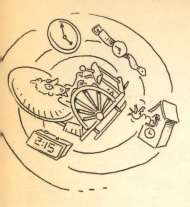

Or if time travel is possible?

Then you have *already* started to grapple with some very famous philosophical puzzles. This book is for those who want to take the next step.

We're going to see if we can figure out the answers to these puzzles by *thinking like detectives*.

So how do detectives think?

When faced with a mystery, Sherlock Holmes would take out his pipe and use his *powers of reason*. He would carefully sift through the evidence and arguments until he was confident he had the answer.

That's how philosophers try to think, too. The idea is coolly and calmly to figure out, as best we can, what's most likely to be true. Of course, we may not be able to solve *all* the mysteries in this book. But I'm pretty sure we will be able to solve *some* of them.

Chapter 1

Astrology, flying saucers and ESP

Mysterious World

Aisha is slumped in an armchair.
She's idly flicking through the
pages of a magazine. Suddenly,
in rushes Tom, one of her
housemates. Tom has been
shopping and is rather excited
about a book he's just bought
from Big Al's Discount
Bookstore. The book is called

Mysterious World and has a large picture of a flying saucer on the
front cover.

Tom: I've got this fantastic book! Take a look. It has lots of great
chapters on weird and spooky stuff: ghosts, alien abductions, the
prophecies of Nostradamus, the Loch Ness monster, astrology,
numerology and palm-reading.

Aisha takes the book and flicks through the pages. She looks unimpressed. In fact she's rather rude about *Mysterious World*.

Aisha: Ah yes. I've seen it. It's a load of rubbish.

Aisha passes *Mysterious World* back to Tom, who seems a little disappointed by her reaction.

Tom: Why do you say that? Shouldn't you be more open-minded?
Aisha: I *am* open-minded.
Tom: But there's plenty of evidence in this book to suggest that there *really is* a lot of weird, paranormal stuff going on in the world. You shouldn't be so dismissive.

Like Tom, many people firmly believe in the kind of things discussed in Tom's book. A great many suppose that by looking to the stars astrologers can predict what will happen and provide us with valuable advice on what we should do.

Some believe in palmistry: they suppose that how your life will go is written on the palm of your hand.

Lots of people claim to have seen ghosts. A surprising number think they have been abducted by aliens. And many people believe in *extra-sensory perception*, or *ESP* – the ability to 'see' what is happening, or even what will happen, without using our five normal senses of sight, touch, taste, smell and hearing.

For example, you occasionally hear tales of people who say they 'just knew' that someone close to them had suffered an accident even though that person was miles away at the time and there was no *normal* way in which they could have known.

It seems it must have been some sort of weird, *paranormal* experience that let them know what happened.

OH NO! RANDY'S HAD A TERRIBLE ACCIDENT!

Many people believe in the paranormal. But, of course, there are also many who don't. Like Aisha, they dismiss claims about astrology, flying saucers and ESP. Sometimes they can be pretty rude. They accuse those who believe in such stuff of being gullible fools.

So what *should* we believe? Is belief in astrology, flying saucers, miracles and ESP a lot of silly superstitious nonsense? Or might there really be something to it?

How open-minded should we be?

Of course, we want to be open-minded. We shouldn't just assume that there's nothing to any of these claims and simply *ignore* the kind of evidence presented in Tom's book.

But, on the other hand, we don't want to be *too* open-minded. We don't want minds *so* open that any old rubbish can easily end up lodging there.

After all, there are so many ridiculous beliefs you might pick up: that the Moon is made out of concrete; that ice is poisonous; that humans have three legs, and so on. If you are too open-minded, your head will soon fill up with junk beliefs.

So let's be open-minded. But let's also try to filter out, as best we can, silly or unreasonable ideas. Let's think hard about the arguments and carefully weigh up the evidence before we allow new beliefs in. That way, there's at least a fair chance that many of our beliefs will be true.

Belief in weird stuff is popular

Let's get back to Tom and Aisha. Why is Tom so confident that there must be something to the claims made in *Mysterious World*?

He begins to flick through the book and comes to a stop at the chapter on astrology.

Tom: OK, what about astrology? It says here that astrology is thousands of years old, and that some of the world's greatest scientists – including even Isaac Newton – have believed in it. Millions of people all over the world use astrology and testify that it *does* work. Even a US President is reported to have consulted an astrologer. Yet *you* confidently dismiss astrology as a load of old rubbish. How can you be so sure?

Tom is right that millions are convinced that astrology can give them an insight into their future. Many claim that they really do 'fit' their astrological star sign. In fact astrology is now a huge industry. Billions of pounds are spent every year on astrologers. Isn't Aisha being far too quick to dismiss astrology as 'rubbish'?

She doesn't think so.

Aisha: Look, I admit that *very many* people, often very intelligent people, believe in astrology. But the fact that lots of people believe something doesn't necessarily give us much reason to believe it's true.

Tom: Doesn't it?

Aisha: No. After all, lots of people *don't* believe in astrology. So you see, e*ither way, lots of people must be wrong.*

Believing what we want to believe

But Tom's point is not just that a great many people believe in astrology. Tom thinks they have *good grounds* for believing in it.

Tom: But surely the reason so many people consult astrologers and have done for thousands of years is that there's plenty of *evidence* that astrology really can give us an insight into the future.

Aisha: So you say. But sometimes people believe something not because there's good evidence that it is true, but for other reasons.

Tom: Like what?

Aisha: Well, sometimes people believe things because they *like* to believe in them. The fact is that we desperately *want* to believe in the weird and wacky. It's exciting to suppose that there are ghosts and demons, that there are cosmic influences shaping our lives, and that we have supernatural powers.

Liars, fakes and charlatans

Tom admits that he would like to believe that the claims made in his book are true. But, as he points out, that doesn't show that they *aren't* true.

Tom: OK, we *want* to believe in the weird and supernatural. But *that doesn't mean there's nothing to it, does it?* And in fact there really is *lots and lots* of evidence of weird and paranormal stuff happening.

Aisha: Is there?

Tom: Certainly. Thousands claim to have witnessed supernatural stuff going on.

Aisha: But many of these people are simply lying!

As Tom points out, it is hardly likely that *all* these people are lying about what they have experienced.

Tom: Well, yes, *some* may be lying. But not all. Many people really do believe they have witnessed something miraculous happening.

Aisha: True. But perhaps they have been *deceived*. There have always been people willing to take advantage of our huge fascination with the weird and wacky. Throughout history there are well-documented cases of tricksters happy to con the gullible by telling them fantastic tales, offering to put them in contact with the dead, selling them 'magical' charms, and so on.

There's little doubt that, even today, a huge amount of fraud and fakery is going on.

It's easy to fake it

Aisha is correct that there are undoubtedly many fakes and charlatans about.

You have probably seen illusionists performing fantastic feats. The magician David Copperfield flies in front of an audience of thousands, apparently without the help of any harness or wires. Others catch bullets in their teeth and cause people to vanish.

Now, as I say, these people are illusionists. They are happy to admit that they engage in trickery and sleight-of-hand. Yet their tricks are at least as convincing as most supposedly 'genuine' cases of the paranormal.

UNCANNY

In fact, it's easy to master highly convincing illusions in just a few hours. A friend of mine recently learnt how to bend spoons. He can even do it without touching them. I have no idea how he does it. Yet he tells me it's all a trick.

Given that it is so easy to master tricks that are just as convincing as the 'genuine' paranormal events, it's highly likely that at least some of these 'genuine' cases are faked too.

Pedlars of tales

As Aisha also points out, there's plenty of money to be made, not just from faking miraculous events, but from re-telling stories about them.

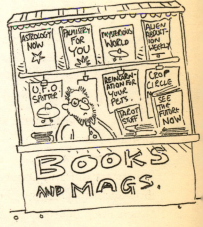

Aisha: Because we *like* to believe in this stuff, there's no shortage of books, magazines, newspapers and TV companies willing to feed our fascination.

Newspapers will always run astrology columns, whether there's anything to astrology or not, simply because they can sell more newspapers that way and so make more money. Television programmes on the weird and wacky can get huge audiences, particularly if they sensationalize reports of fantastic things happening and give little time to anyone who wants to look at the evidence more critically.

Twisting the tale

Aisha is right that people usually have an interest – sometimes a financial interest – in telling tales of the supernatural. That should lead us to treat their 'evidence' with caution.

Another reason he should handle such tales with care is that they often reach us third- or fourth-hand. People may think they are telling the story just as it was told to them. But it's still easy for the story to become embellished along the way. The storyteller is likely to focus on those aspects of their story that are most amazing, and to play down any features that would make it seem less fantastic. A report of a 'strange light in the sky' can quickly become a tale of alien abduction.

Aisha sums up her case:

Aisha: So it seems to me it's not at all surprising that there are these reports of the weird and supernatural in our newspapers and on television. In fact, given our gullibility, the ease with which we can be taken for a ride, the extent to which stories can evolve along the way, and the huge profits to be made from telling them, you would expect such reports *anyway*, whether or not there was any truth to them. *So the mere fact that there are so many reports gives us little if any reason to suppose they are true.*

Is Aisha right?

Tom's stars

Tom accepts that many of the reports concerning weird and supernatural goings-on probably are unreliable. But he remains convinced that it's still *perfectly reasonable* to believe in astrology, flying saucers and ESP.

Tom: Look, I admit that there are fakes and charlatans. I admit that there's lots of money to be made peddling dubious stories about astrology, ESP, ghosts and so on. But that doesn't explain away *all* the evidence we have for these things, does it?

Aisha: It doesn't?

Tom: No. We also have *good, solid* evidence.

Aisha: Give me an example of this good, solid evidence.

Tom: Well, my *own* experiences confirm that astrology really does work. So I don't need to rely on the testimony of others.

Tom starts to tell Aisha about his recent experience of an astrological prediction 'coming true'.

Tom: I'm a Sagittarian. Last Monday I read in the astrology column that I could expect a pay rise. And this week I got a pay rise. So you see, there's a piece of evidence that astrology works! And this bit of evidence doesn't come from a dubious source. It's based on what I have experienced *myself*.

Many who believe in the power of astrology can point to countless such examples of astrological predictions turning out to be correct. How are astrologers able to make all these correct predictions if astrology doesn't work?

Making vague predictions

Aisha scratches her head.

Aisha: Let's take a closer look at your evidence. You say this astrological prediction was in Monday's paper?

Aisha rummages in the pile of papers beside the sofa and pulls out Monday's. Then she starts to rifle through the pages.

Aisha: Ah, here we are. 'The Great Magica's predictions for the next week. Sagittarius. Next week brings good news and bad. A friend feels betrayed, and there may be some hostility. Honesty is the best policy. At work things are looking up. You will soon be rewarded for all your hard work.'

Tom: See? It says I'll soon be rewarded for all my hard work. And this week my boss gave me a rise. The Great Magica knew I would get a pay rise!

SAGITTARIUS
NEXT WEEK BRINGS
GOOD NEWS AND BAD.
A FRIEND FEELS
BETRAYED, AND THERE
MAY BE SOME HOSTILITY.
HONESTY IS THE BEST
POLICY. AT WORK
THINGS ARE LOOKING
UP. YOU WILL SOON BE
REWARDED FOR ALL
YOUR HARD WORK.

But *did* she? What do you think?

The Great Magica's predictions are pretty *vague*, aren't they? She doesn't actually say that every Sagittarian will get a pay rise. She says only that there will be a 'reward' for hard work. But she never specifically mentions money. This means that, even if Tom had received a box of chocolates or a day off from his boss, the Great Magica's prediction would still have come true.

It would also have come true if he had managed to sell more cars than usual. That too might count as a 'reward'.

In fact, the astrologer's prediction could be seen as 'true' if Tom had received a tip or even just praise from a grateful customer.

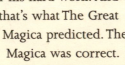

Still, Tom did get a reward for his hard work. And that's what The Great Magica predicted. The Great Magica was correct.

So did she really know what would happen?

How astrology columns *really* work

No. She didn't. Newspaper astrology columns don't provide us with any sort of insight into the future. Aisha explains how they *really* work.

Aisha: Look, you read the astrology column every week. Every week Magica makes a number of rather vague predictions. Now because her predictions are vague – because there are so many different ways in which they could 'come true' – you should actually expect quite a few of them to 'come true' just by chance.

Aisha is right. But then the fact that one of the Great Magica's vague predictions came true this week doesn't give us the slightest reason to suppose that astrology gives her some strange power to see into the future.

Aisha: Also, notice that the Great Magica made a *number* of predictions for Sagittarians. For example, she said "A friend feels betrayed, and there may be some hostility. Honesty is the best policy."

Tom: True, she did.

Aisha: But you have just ignored *this* prediction, haven't you?

Tom: Er, yes, I suppose I have.

Aisha: Why?

Tom: To be honest, I forgot about that one. It doesn't seem to have come true.

Aisha: Right, because you don't immediately see how it applies to you, *you ignore it.* In fact, some weeks you can't find *anything* in the Great Magica's predictions that rings true, can you?

Tom: Well, yes, *some* weeks I can't. But she usually gets *something* right!

Aisha is getting pretty exasperated.

Aisha: Of course she does! Because the Great Magica makes loads of vague predictions, she is bound to get a *few* right *just by chance*. Readers remember when a prediction comes true – that's not surprising, of course, because it's quite dramatic: it seems the astrologer 'knew' what would happen! Readers also tend to forget about the predictions that *don't* come true – again, that's not surprising as nothing happens later on to remind them about the prediction. So you see, by focusing only on the 'hits' and forgetting about the 'misses', gullible people like you can convince yourselves that the Great Magica has some sort of magical insight into the future!

An astrology experiment

Perhaps you aren't convinced by Aisha's explanation of how astrology columns work. Perhaps you still think there's *something* to it.

If you do, then try this simple test. Cut out the predictions for the twelve different star signs from last week's newspaper. Make a note of which prediction is for which star sign, and then remove the star signs so that only the predictions are left, like this:

NEXT WEEK BRINGS GOOD NEWS AND BAD. A FRIEND FEELS BETRAYED, AND THERE MAY BE SOME HOSTILITY. HONESTY IS THE BEST POLICY. AT WORK THINGS ARE LOOKING UP. YOU WILL SOON BE REWARDED FOR ALL YOUR HARD WORK

Now show your friends just the predictions and ask them which prediction is for their star sign.

If the astrologer has *any* sort of insight into the future, then your friends should have a better than one-in-twelve chance of picking out the prediction that's for their sign. But in fact, your friends won't be able to figure out which predictions are theirs. Because the predictions are so vague, they will probably find that most of the predictions have 'come true' for them.

Try it and see.

Astrological charts

Of course, many astrologers admit that the kind of predictions that appear in newspapers and magazines are just 'a bit of fun'. Most astrologers would say that a *proper* astrological chart, based on specific information about a person's date and time of birth, is likely to be much more reliable.

But is this true?

In 1979, a researcher into astrology put an advert in a magazine offering free personal horoscopes. Each person who answered the advert received a real horoscope drawn up by a reputable astrologer. When someone received their free horoscope, they were also asked how accurate they and their friends found it to be.

Amazingly, of the first 150 people who responded, 94% said their horoscope was accurate, and 90% of their friends and family thought it accurate too.

Doesn't *this* show that personal horoscopes *really are* accurate?

No, it doesn't. True, in this experiment everyone received a real astrological chart drawn up by a real astrologer. But it was the *very same* horoscope each time. They all got a chart based on the birth details of the notorious mass murderer Dr Petiot, who was executed in 1947. Petiot admitted killing 63 people and dissolving their bodies in a tub of quicklime!

Yet 94% of the people given Petiot's chart were convinced that the chart accurately described them!

14

'YOU ENJOY MEETING NEW PEOPLE AND ARE ALWAYS CURIOUS ABOUT WHAT'S GOING ON INSIDE THEM.' Hmmm, THAT SOUNDS JUST LIKE ME!

What this case again shows is that most of us are easily duped into thinking that astrologers know things about us that they couldn't possibly know if astrology didn't work. The fact is it's incredibly easy for us to convince ourselves that astrologers are accurate no matter what they might happen to say.

Flying saucers

Tom still thinks that Aisha is being far too quick to rubbish *everything* in *Mysterious World*.

Tom: OK. So you don't believe in astrology. But surely you're wrong to be sceptical about *all* the things discussed in this book. What about flying saucers and alien abductions, for example? Just two years ago, an accountant was taken up into a flying saucer.

He reports having been subjected to strange internal examinations.

Then the aliens dropped him off in some woods in the middle of the night.

Aisha: Hmm.

Tom: Thousands of people have witnessed such things. *Thousands* have seen flying saucers in the sky. They can't *all* be deluded, can they?

Tom thinks it's totally unreasonable to dismiss *all* this evidence. Yet Aisha is *still* sceptical.

Aisha: I don't think there's enough evidence to make it sensible to believe that people are abducted by flying saucers.

Tom: But there's lots of hard evidence too. What about the *films* and *photographs* of flying saucers?

Aisha: Many have been exposed as fakes. One of the most famous turned out to be a car hubcap. And why is it that the pictures are *always* fuzzy and difficult to make out? Out of all the thousands and thousands of photographs that have been taken of UFOs, why isn't there even *one* nice, clear picture of a flying saucer?

THAT'S RIGHT SON, FLING IT IN THE AIR!

Tom: Well, it's often dark. People are excited. It's not surprising if the camera shakes a bit. But look, even if the pictures *aren't* that great, the people who took them know what they saw.

Aisha: Do they? Let me tell you about the very first flying saucer.

The very first flying saucer

Aisha: It was way back in 1947. Kenneth Arnold, an American pilot, was flying his plane in broad daylight. It was a routine flight. Visibility was good. There was nothing out of the ordinary. Then, suddenly, Arnold spotted nine strange flying objects. On returning to the airfield, Arnold described what he had seen. It wasn't long before his report of 'flying saucers' had been transmitted across the country. The press went wild!

Soon, others started to see saucers, and of course the rest is history. We've been seeing these strange, saucer-shaped craft in the sky ever since. Flying saucers have since been immortalized in countless stories and films, including *Close Encounters of the Third Kind, Men in Black* and *The Day the Earth Stood Still.*

Tom: But if there have been many thousands of reports of flying saucers, many from highly qualified pilots, why don't you believe they exist?

Aisha smiles wryly.

Aisha: Because I know that *Arnold didn't see flying saucers.*
Tom: He didn't?
Aisha: No. He never said he saw saucers. Arnold said that the craft he saw looked like *boomerangs.*

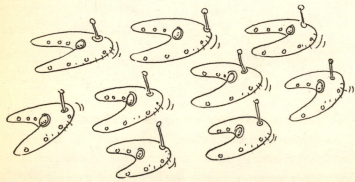

Tom: Boomerangs?

Aisha: That's right. He merely said that they *flew* like saucers would if skipped across a lake. They sort of bounced along.

Tom: Oh.

Aisha: But in the excitement that followed the sighting, that particular detail was lost. Arnold was reported as having seen saucers. Now think about it: why have there been thousands of reports of flying *saucers* since 1947, if what Arnold saw did not look like saucers but boomerangs?

Tom: Hmm. That's a good question.

Aisha: What's more likely? That some of the reports of saucers made since 1947 have been reliable, it's just that back in 1947 the aliens coincidentally happened to change the shape of the spacecraft from boomerang to saucer?

Or that the reports of saucers since 1947 are actually a result of the *power of suggestion.*

Tom: Power of suggestion?

Aisha: Yes. People saw a distant plane or a cloud or a meteor or a bright star or some other vague light in the sky, or merely

19

hallucinated, and, because they *expected* an alien craft to be saucer-shaped, they subconsciously turned what they saw into a saucer.
Tom: Well, I guess that *is* the more likely explanation.

Tom is right. Our tendency to 'see' whatever we strongly want or expect to see has been studied extensively by scientists. The only even half-plausible explanation for the thousands of flying saucer reports made since 1947 is that they are down to the power of suggestion.

Of course, the fact that the accountant who claimed to have been abducted by aliens said he was kidnapped by a *flying saucer* also tends to undermine his credibility. What is more likely, that the accountant really was taken up by a flying saucer, or that he had a vivid dream, hallucinated or made the whole thing up?

Surely it's much more plausible that he is either deluded or else is deliberately deceiving us.

'Seeing' things

Of course, you will already be familiar with the power of the mind to 'see' things that aren't there.

Have you ever lain on your back and watched the clouds scud by? It's possible to 'see' all sorts of things in them: faces, animals, cars, countries...

…or perhaps you have sat in bed and watched as your dressing-gown transformed itself into a hideous creature.

The more you stare, the more real the creature seems, until you can almost convince yourself it is real.

I have 'heard' faint voices in the hiss of my TV set.

I have also become absolutely convinced I could smell a gas leak, when in fact there wasn't any gas at all.

The Mars face

In fact, our ability to 'see' things that aren't there partly explains one recent mystery: the Mars face. In 1976, the space probe Viking Orbiter 1 was taking pictures of the Cydonia region of Mars. On 25th July it photographed what appeared to be a huge alien face carved into the surface of the planet.

Many people believe that the face is a sculpture created by an alien race in their own image.

Certainly, the face does look a bit reptilian.

But the truth is that the face is actually a rather lumpy hill that, when lit from a certain angle, happens to cast shadows that resemble a face.

There are many thousands of hills, craters and other features on the surface of Mars. You would *expect* to find, just by chance, one or two that resemble familiar things. And because it is *particularly* easy for us to 'see' randomly arranged blobs and shadows as faces (faces are one of the easiest things to 'see' in clouds and campfires, for example) it isn't terribly surprising that a 'face' was discovered on the surface of Mars.

So the Mars face is really a result of two things: our ability to 'see' things as faces combined with the probability that a face-like combination of blobs and shadows would show up somewhere or other on the surface of a nearby planet.

I'm afraid the Mars face provides little evidence of an alien race. We can similarly explain why, every now and then, someone cuts open a piece of fruit that appears to contain a piece of writing or an image of someone.
Cut open enough pieces of fruit and eventually you are going to find a face-like combination of pips just by chance.

Miracles

Let's get back to Tom and Aisha. Tom has moved on to the chapter of *Mysterious World* that focuses on miracles.

Tom: OK. What about miracles?
Aisha: Miracles?
Tom: Yes. It says here that every day, fantastic things happen. Statues start to weep. People are suddenly cured of fatal diseases.

Tom pointed to the page in front of him.

Tom: Here's a particularly good example. A couple of years ago, in South America, a train went out of control. It was just about to crash into a station full of people, killing hundreds.

But at the last moment the points in front of the train failed, sending it harmlessly off on to another track.

Now how do you explain *that*? The points failed at the precise moment the runaway train came along! Obviously, that wasn't just a coincidence. Someone or something must have acted from 'beyond' to divert the train. It was a *miracle*!

Aisha: You mean God, or some other sort of supernatural being, lent a helping hand?

Tom: Exactly!

The power of coincidence

In fact, Aisha is happy to admit that a sort of 'miracle' happened.

Aisha: I agree. There *was* a 'miracle'. But only in the sense that there was a very happy *coincidence*. I don't see that there's much reason to suppose that some sort of supernatural being intervened.

Tom: Why not? You can't *seriously* maintain this was just a coincidence, can you?

Aisha: Yes I can. It almost certainly was just a coincidence. Look, there are *billions* of people all over the Earth, each one of whom has many thousands of experiences each day.

Tom: True.

Aisha: Now with *that* many people around experiencing that many things, some are bound to experience some pretty fantastic coincidences. Millions of people will be *very, very* lucky during their lifetime. Thousands will be stupendously lucky, perhaps having their life saved by a truly amazing coincidence. Hundreds will be so lucky as to be almost beyond belief. One or two will have good luck of such mind-wrenchingly, gob-smackingly awesome proportions that most of us simply won't be able to believe or comprehend just how lucky they have been.

Tom: Hmm. I *guess* that's true.

Aisha: Yet now you point to one case of fantastic good luck and say 'See, that shows there must be some sort of supernatural intervention involved!' Well, you're wrong. It doesn't. I'm afraid you have simply underestimated just how much amazing good fortune we should *expect* to find in the world.

I think Aisha is right. In fact, it would be truly peculiar if some people *didn't* get stupendously lucky every now and then. That really *would* be evidence for some sort of supernatural intervention.

Extra-Sensory Perception

Tom flips forward a few pages and comes to the chapter on psychics.

Tom: Ah. Then what about psychics? There's a great deal of evidence that they really do have some sort of weird, paranormal power. Even my auntie is convinced.

Aisha: She is?

Tom: Yes. A few weeks ago, her psychic told her that she had an uncle called 'Harold' who had a slipped disc and died of a heart attack. Yet my Auntie had *never even mentioned* Harold before. How could Auntie's psychic have known these details if she didn't have the gift of extra- sensory perception?

Tom is right that this sort of testimony about the powers of psychics is very common. Doesn't it provide us with pretty good evidence that extra-sensory perception (or ESP) really exists?

Perhaps. But before we make up our minds, let's look a little more closely at what *really* happened when Tom's auntie visited her psychic.

Auntie's visit to the psychic

Auntie enters a dimly lit room. The psychic is sitting at a table with a crystal ball.

Psychic: Hello, dearie. Do sit down.

Auntie: Thank you.

Psychic: Now... I'm getting a name.

The room goes deathly quiet.

Psychic: Henry... or Harold...?
Auntie: Uncle Harold?
Psychic: Yes, that's right! Hmm... I'm sensing some back trouble.
Auntie: Amazing! He slipped a disc just before he died.

The psychic waves towards the middle of her chest.

Psychic: Am I right in thinking it was trouble *here* that killed him?
Auntie: How did you know? It was a heart attack!
Psychic: Yes, yes. That's right. He just told me it was his ticker that got
   him in the end.

Auntie thinks that her psychic knew she had an uncle called
'Harold' who had a slipped disc and died of a heart attack.

Certainly, you can see why Auntie believes her psychic has
genuine psychic powers. But let's look a little more closely at
what the psychic *actually* says.

How the psychic fooled Auntie

The psychic begins with a name: Henry. Then she leaves a pause.
She gets no response from Auntie, so she tries another name:
Harold. This time it's a name Auntie recognizes.

But notice that most people of Auntie's age are likely to know
people with one or other of these two names (try asking anyone
over the age of 60 whether they know, or knew, anyone with
either name – I bet they do). So the fact that Auntie recognizes
one of the two names is hardly surprising.

Also notice that the psychic doesn't say that Auntie's *uncle* was
called 'Harold'. Actually, it is Auntie who gives the psychic that
piece of information. The psychic merely asks if either name
means anything to Auntie.

So far, *the psychic hasn't told Auntie anything at all.*

What happens next? The psychic says she senses 'back trouble'. But notice how very vague this statement is. The psychic doesn't say whom this back trouble is supposed to afflict. It could be Auntie's back that she's talking about. Or Harold's. Or some other person known to Auntie. Or it could be a *prediction* of back trouble to come. As almost everyone suffers from back pain at some point or another, it's not particularly surprising that Uncle Harold had back trouble himself.

Also notice that the psychic doesn't say *what sort* of back trouble she has in mind. Again, it is Auntie who tells the psychic about Harold's slipped disc, not the other way round.

So the psychic still hasn't given Auntie any information. In fact *it is Auntie who's providing all the information.*

Then the psychic asks if Harold died from trouble somewhere in the chest area. Notice that she doesn't *claim* that he did. She merely *asks* if he did. And remember that Auntie has already told the psychic that Harold is dead. Notice that, if Harold didn't die from trouble in the chest area, the psychic can still stress that she was merely *asking*, and hasn't yet made a mistake. But as almost *everyone* does die from trouble in the chest area in the end (even diseases of the head and limbs usually kill by travelling to organs in the torso), it was hardly surprising that poor old Harold went the same way.

Notice that when Auntie tells the psychic that Harold died of a heart attack, the psychic claims this was *something she knew already.* But what evidence is there that she did?

So far, *none at all.*

28

I have based Auntie's conversation with her psychic on some real conversations with psychics. This example illustrates just one or two of the very many techniques that psychics can use to convince people that they have genuinely psychic powers.

Though Auntie believes her psychic knew various details about her uncle Harold, it turns out that it was Auntie who supplied all the information. By making vague claims, asking questions and fishing for information the psychic cleverly managed the conversation to make it seem as if she was actually communicating with Auntie's dead uncle.

Of course, I am not suggesting that all psychics *deliberately* trick their customers. Most psychics really believe they have psychic powers. They don't just manage to convince other people of their paranormal gifts. They end up convincing themselves too.

Perhaps some psychics really do have genuinely psychic powers. But the fact that thousands of people are taken in by this sort of conversation on a regular basis doesn't really provide much evidence that they do.

The strange case of Clever Hans

Psychics may not just be using trickery to create the illusion that they have paranormal powers. They may also be reading very subtle clues in their customers' behaviour.

Let me tell you the true story of the horse Clever Hans.

Back in 1888, Hans's owner decided that he would try to teach Hans maths. After a great deal of careful training, Hans was eventually able to tap out with his hoof the answer to mathematical questions. For example, ask Hans 'What is twelve divided by four?' and Hans would tap his hoof three times.

Hans could perform even without his trainer present. There was no deliberate trickery involved: Hans's owner believed his horse really could do maths.

Clever Hans soon become world-famous, his abilities baffling both scientists and public audiences alike.

So could Hans *really* do maths?

No. He couldn't. Eventually, a young psychologist tested whether Hans could still perform if asked the questions by someone who didn't know the answers. It turned out he couldn't.

Somehow, Hans was reading tiny changes in the behaviour of his questioners, tapping his foot until some unconscious cue – such as a slight tensing of the questioner's body – told him when to stop. Someone who didn't know the answers was unable to supply Hans with these cues, which is why Hans then lost his mathematical powers.

What moral should we draw from this tale? Well, if a horse can learn to read such subtle, unconsciously-given signals, then no doubt a psychic can too. It may be that many psychics have learnt – perhaps without realizing that this is what they are doing – to read the same sorts of cues in their customers' behaviour. While impressive, there would be nothing spooky and supernatural about such an ability.

So it turns out that there are all sorts of perfectly normal ways in which psychics might convince their customers that they have supernatural powers.

A less than mysterious conclusion

Tom puts *Mysterious World* down on the coffee table. It lands with a thump.

Tom is feeling rather frustrated. Despite coming up with what seem to him to be perfectly good reasons for believing in astrology, flying saucers and ESP, Aisha remains entirely unconvinced.

Tom: Look, you can't *prove* that there are no flying saucers. You can't *prove* that there's nothing to astrology.

Aisha: Well, if you mean there's *some* room for doubt, then, yes, I admit I can't prove we aren't visited by flying saucers. My point is that there just isn't anything like the evidence needed to make it *reasonable* to believe in such things.

Tom: But shouldn't you be open-minded?

Aisha: I am open-minded in the sense that I am perfectly willing to look at any new evidence that might come along. But the fact remains that there's *very little reason* to suppose that we are visited by flying saucers, and so on. The evidence for saucers is extremely suspect. Mostly it takes the form of *testimony*: people tell about seeing saucers, meeting aliens, being abducted. But there's plenty of reason to distrust this testimony, isn't there? In fact, given our fascination with flying saucers, the ease with which we can be fooled, the power of suggestion, the way in which tales can become embellished, and the money to be made from peddling such tales, we really should *expect* a great deal of testimony *anyway*, whether or not there's anything to it.

Tom: But you admit there *might* be something to it?

Aisha: Yes. It *might* be true

GEE, IT SEEMS TO BE MADE OF ... CONCRETE!

SSSSH! DON'T TELL ANYONE! THEY'll NEVER BELIEVE US.

that we are visited by flying saucers. It *might* be true that some people have psychic powers. But then it *might* be true that the moon is made of concrete...

... that French people are really from Pluto...

... and that George W. Bush is Elvis Presley with plastic surgery.

It *might* be true. That's not to deny that the evidence really doesn't support *any* of these claims. So it's downright irrational of you to believe them. *All* of them.

Is Aisha being fair?

In this chapter I have given you plenty of reasons for being *careful* about accepting evidence of weird, supernatural things happening. But it's up to you to figure out whether there is, after all, enough good evidence to make it reasonable to believe such things happen. Perhaps there is.

What do you think?

Chapter 2

Killing people

It's wrong to kill

We all know that killing is wrong. In fact we think of killing as one of the very worst things a person can do. But is it *always* wrong to kill? Are there any exceptions to the rule?

Obviously, we think it's fine to kill bacteria and viruses. And we are happy about killing plants, especially if we are going to eat them.

Generally speaking, we think there is nothing wrong with killing these sorts of living thing.

Many also believe it's OK to kill *animals* (though of course not everyone agrees about that). Where I live, the majority think it's morally acceptable to kill and eat pigs, cows and chickens for food. Most people are also willing to annihilate insects, slugs and snails, particularly if they are eating our cabbages.

So when we say 'It's wrong to kill', it's clear we don't mean it to apply to *all* living things. In fact it seems we really only mean it to apply to *other people*.

In this chapter, I am going to look at the question of whether there are any exceptions to the rule that we shouldn't kill other people. Is it always wrong to take another person's life? Or are there some situations in which it *is* morally acceptable?

Capital punishment

Let's start with the death penalty, otherwise known as capital punishment.

While almost everyone believes it is wrong to kill other people, many make an exception for murderers. They think that the death penalty is an acceptable punishment for those guilty of deliberately killing another person.

A number of countries have the death penalty, including Saudi Arabia and the United States. Murderers and other criminals have been put to death by hanging, beheading, electrocution, shooting, lethal injection, or gas.

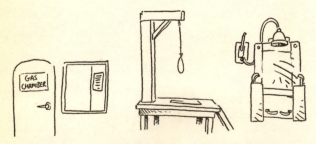

But is it *really* morally acceptable for us to kill murderers? Should we consider them an exception to the rule?

As you are about to discover, Carol certainly thinks so.

Stringing up Dick Rotten

Carol and Aisha are watching the news on TV.

The newsreader has just reported that in the US the murderer Dick Rotten has finally been executed after spending six years on death row.

Carol is delighted.

Carol: Hooray! And about time too.

Aisha is a little surprised at Carol.

Aisha: Why are you so happy? Someone's just been *killed*! It's wrong to take another person's life.
Carol: Always?
Aisha: Yes. There's *never* an excuse. There was no *need* to kill Dick Rotten. They could have put him in jail instead.

Getting your own back

Carol admits that they didn't *need* to kill Dick Rotten.

Carol: True, they didn't have to kill him. But Rotten killed somebody else, didn't he? He murdered an innocent woman. So *justice has been done*! He's been killed in return.

There's no doubt that this is the way many people think about the death penalty. It's right to execute murderers: they're simply getting what's coming to them.

But Aisha thinks this is a very childish attitude to take.

Aisha: That's a brutal way of looking at life, isn't it? It's the morality of the school playground. Someone does something to you, so you do it to them! Remember when we were at school and Mary poked me in the eye?

I poked *her* right back.

Now I got told off for behaving like that, didn't I?

Carol: Yes, you did. Miss Tick was very cross. She said that two wrongs don't make a right.

Aisha: So why is it OK for *adults* to take revenge? Why is it right for them to kill the killer? I don't think it is.

The Bible

Carol suggests that perhaps the Bible can be used to justify the death penalty.

Carol: But what about 'an eye for an eye'? That's what it says in the Old Testament, isn't it? Surely we are *entitled* to get our own back.

Aisha: But why not quote from the New Testament, where Saint Paul very clearly says that we should not return evil for evil, but 'leave vengeance for God'?

And remember that one of the Ten Commandments is simply 'Do not kill'. It doesn't say 'Do not kill, *except for murderers*', does it?

Aisha is correct: the Bible doesn't appear to support the death penalty.

Aisha: It just seems to me that taking a life is wrong, *no matter what.* Killing is wrong, *full stop.*

Two arguments for the death penalty

We have seen that Aisha believes there are absolutely no exceptions to the rule that we shouldn't kill other people. So she thinks it is wrong to kill murderers.

Still, perhaps there are good reasons why at least some murderers should be executed. Can you think of any?

Carol thinks hard. After a minute or so, she comes up with a couple of arguments which she thinks do justify capital punishment. In fact, they are probably the two most popular arguments for the death penalty.

Let's look at the arguments one at a time and try to figure out whether they are any good.

Here's the first.

Argument one: deterrence

Carol begins by arguing that, by executing some murderers, we will *deter* others from committing the same crime.

Carol: What about *deterrence*?

Aisha: You mean, people will think twice before murdering someone if they believe they may face a death sentence?

Carol: Exactly.

Aisha: But isn't prison a deterrent too? People will also be afraid of committing murder if they think they're likely to be locked up for years and years.

Carol: But the deterrent effect of the death penalty is *stronger*. So, if we have the death penalty for murder, *innocent lives will be saved*.

At first sight, the deterrence argument looks pretty plausible. If capital punishment saves innocent lives, isn't that a *very* good reason for having it?

Is the death penalty a stronger deterrent than prison?

Aisha is not convinced.

Aisha: Trouble is, I'm not sure the death penalty *is* a stronger deterrent than jail. If it was, then you would expect countries with the death penalty to have lower murder rates, right?

Aisha: But actually, countries with the death penalty *don't* usually have lower murder rates. Compare the United States and Western Europe. Many states in the US have the death penalty. No Western European country does. Yet the murder rate is actually much higher in the US than it is in Western Europe.

Carol: Oh.

Aisha: And when we look inside America, we find that those states that have the death penalty tend not to have the lowest murder rate, but the highest! Like Texas.

Carol looks irritated.

Carol: But hang on a minute. Maybe the reason Texas has the death penalty is *because* of its higher murder rate, rather than the other way round.

Aisha: What do you mean?

Carol: Well, perhaps, because it has a problem with murder, Texas thinks it needs to introduce the death penalty. In fact, I bet the murder rate would be *even higher* if Texas didn't have capital punishment!

Aisha's eyes narrow.

Aisha: But again, that's not what the evidence suggests. Studies have repeatedly failed to show any deterrent effect. When states introduce the death penalty, as often as not the murder rate *goes up*. And when they *stop* executing, as often as not, the murder rate *falls*.

What Aisha says is true: it's not at all clear that execution does act as a stronger deterrent than a heavy prison sentence.

For example, when California carried out an execution every other month (between 1952 and 1967), murder rates increased

10% annually, on average. Between 1967 and 1991, when there were no executions in California, the murder rate increased by only 4.8% annually.

Of course, figures like these should always be treated with caution. With a little careful selection it's easy to make the evidence show whatever you want it to show. But perhaps it's worth mentioning that a survey of experts – from the American Society of Criminology, the Law and Society Association and the Academy of Criminal Justice Sciences – showed the overwhelming majority did not believe the death penalty to be 'a proven deterrent to murder'. These people will have looked very closely at the evidence and will be in a particularly good position to judge.

The 'common sense' justification

Still, you might think it pretty obvious that the death penalty must be a stronger deterrent than jail.

Why is that? Well, ask most people what they would prefer, death or a long stretch in jail, and I'm sure they would choose jail. Jail would be considered less awful (though still pretty

awful, of course).

So isn't it just *common sense* that the death penalty is a stronger deterrent?

Maybe not. To begin with, the death penalty will only act as a significantly stronger deterrent than a prison sentence if the murderer thinks they are likely to be caught. What about those calculating murderers who carefully weigh up the consequences before committing their crime? Presumably, these people only commit murder because they think it highly unlikely they'll be convicted. But then the death penalty isn't going to put them off much more than a long jail term. Neither is much of a deterrent if you're pretty confident you're going to get away with it.

BUT IF WE GET CAUGHT, WE'll BE SENTENCED TO DEATH!

WHO CARES? WE AREN'T GOING TO GET CAUGHT!

What, then, about the rest: those who commit murder without considering the consequences? Some murders are committed in a frenzy of panic or hatred. The murderer lashes out in a blind fury without thinking at all. But if these people don't bother to weigh up the consequences, then the death penalty is hardly likely to put them off killing either.

So while the death penalty may deter *some* people, it probably won't be very many. And where the death penalty does deter more than jail, it probably won't be by very much. And, as we have seen, when we look at the statistics, that is exactly what they appear to bear out.

So, despite its popularity, the deterrence argument for the death penalty turns out, on closer inspection, to be a rather bad argument.

Argument two: the murderer cannot kill again

Carol decides to give up on the deterrence argument. She moves on to her second argument.

Carol: OK, here's another reason why we should have the death penalty for murder. By killing the murderer, *you prevent them killing again.*

Carol is, of course, perfectly correct: you can hardly go out and murder more people if you're dead.

Carol: You must have read that newspaper report about the murderer Evil Bert. He was recently released. And he immediately went out and killed ten more people!

Aisha: I know. It was a shocking case.

Carol: So you see? If Evil Bert had been executed, innocent lives would have been saved! What's more important, the life of a murdering monster like Evil Bert, or the lives of his future victims?

Carol is correct: a number of released murderers have killed again. Isn't this a good reason to execute them instead?

Aisha doesn't think so.

Ashia: You haven't succeeded in justifying the death penalty, I'm afraid. For of course the *other* option was to lock Evil Bert up and throw away the key. If we lock someone up for life, then they can't kill again, can they?

Carol: Well, I suppose not.

Aisha: Maybe it's true that certain murderers should *never* be released. Obviously to release Evil Bert was a mistake. It doesn't follow that it's best if murderers are executed, does it?

Carol has to admit that it doesn't follow. We could just keep them permanently locked up. In fact, in the US courts already have this option.

Justifying exceptions to the rule

We have been looking at what are probably the two most popular arguments for capital punishment. The first argument is that the death penalty saves innocent lives by deterring would-be murderers. The second is that if we kill murderers we will save innocent lives by preventing them from killing again. We have seen that, when examined more closely, neither argument is particularly convincing.

Now my *own* view – and of course you may not agree with me: you should think this through for yourself and make up your own mind – is that unless we can come up with some pretty good reason why we should execute murderers, then we shouldn't execute them.

Why do I think that? Well, we all admit that, *generally speaking*, it's wrong to take another person's life. We all sign up to that general rule, don't we – even those of us who favour the death penalty?

But if we all accept it's generally wrong to kill another human being, then it is up to those who favour the death penalty to explain why killing murderers is an exception to the rule. It's not up to opponents of the death penalty to explain why it isn't.

The bottom line is this: we all accept that it's wrong to kill anyone unless there is very good reason to do so. So we shouldn't kill murderers unless we can come up with a very good reason to do so.

So far, we haven't seen any particularly good reasons why we should execute murderers. So, unless Carol can come up with a better reason for executing them (and perhaps she can), I think she should accept that we shouldn't execute them.

An argument against the death penalty

Let's now take a look at one of the most popular arguments *against* capital punishment.

In the United Kingdom capital punishment was abolished back in 1965. One popular argument against reintroducing the death penalty is that innocent people would almost certainly end up being executed. Since capital punishment was abolished there have been a number of famous cases in which innocent people were convicted of murder. The mistake was discovered and these innocent people are now free.

But if the UK still had the death penalty for murder, these innocent people would all be dead. The injustice done to them could never be rectified.

So it is clear that, *because the UK doesn't have the death penalty, a number of innocent lives have been saved.*

There's also little doubt that in the US *innocent people continue to be executed.* Since 1973, 102 prisoners have been released from death row in the USA after evidence of their innocence emerged. Some came very close to execution after spending many years under sentence of death. This suggests that, in all probability, a number of people have been executed who were innocent.

Of course, some might say that this shows, not that murderers shouldn't be executed, but that the US legal system needs to be improved so that fewer innocent people are convicted of murder.

Still, there's little doubt that, if we have the death penalty, some innocent people are inevitably going to be executed no matter how careful we are. Is that a price worth paying for having the death penalty? What do you think?

Making up your own mind

As I say, I am not in favour of the death penalty. It seems to me that when we look at the arguments carefully they turn out clearly to support the abolition of capital punishment.

But of course, I make mistakes. Perhaps you disagree with me. Maybe you can come up with better arguments for the death penalty. You might even be able to find a fatal flaw in the popular argument against the death penalty.

We all have a duty to think for ourselves and make up our own minds about whether or not it's right to execute murderers. Don't just uncritically accept what I happen to think.

Executions are fun!

But do be careful that you don't simply give in to the desire for vengeance.

Let me admit something. There are bad people in the world who, frankly, I would really rather *enjoy* seeing executed. Yes, that's right: even though I have argued against the death penalty, a part of me still says, 'Let's string Dick Rotten up! Let's strap Evil Bert to the electric chair!'

Action movies often appeal to such feelings. We love to watch the villain get his come-uppance in the final scene, dying in

some particularly gruesome way.
It's highly satisfying to watch the
evil fiend get impaled on a huge
metal spike.

We all have these
feelings. They're perfectly
natural. We shouldn't be *too*
ashamed of them.

But you should be wary of automatically giving in to them, of
assuming that if you *feel good* about what is happening, then it *is
good*.

While the death penalty has many supporters, it seems to me
that, for some, the real motivation is that they feel angry and
want vengeance. They enjoy the idea of the murderer being
killed. They want to see him writhe and squirm in agony, just as
his victim did.

But I'm afraid these feelings don't justify capital punishment. The fact that we rather enjoy killing murderers doesn't make it morally acceptable.

Killing the guilty in defence of the innocent

We have seen that Aisha thinks it's *always* wrong to take another person's life no matter what. She thinks there are absolutely no exceptions to this rule.

I agree with Aisha that we shouldn't execute murderers. But I am not so sure that there are *no* exceptions.

Carol now comes up with an interesting case.

Carol: OK, perhaps it's true that we shouldn't kill murderers. But it's not *always* wrong to kill.

Aisha: Why not?

Carol: Suppose that Evil Bert runs into your home carrying a gun. It's clear he's going to murder you and your family.

AND NOW I'M GOING TO KILL YOU ALL ... HA HA HA !

Now suppose you have a gun, and that you know the only way to stop Evil Bert is by shooting him dead. What should you do?

PAH ! YOU'll NEVER SHOOT ! AND NOW YOU DIE !!!

Aisha: Shoot Bert dead, I guess.

Carol: Right. But then you think that it *is* OK to kill another human being in this sort of case.

Aisha: Hmm. I guess so. Killing someone who's about to murder innocent people is morally acceptable if that's the only way to stop them. But that's the only exception to the rule that we should not kill.

Almost everyone agrees that this really is a legitimate exception to the rule: do not kill. Surely it would be wrong to stand back and let Evil Bert slaughter an innocent family, even if the only way to stop him is by killing him.

So it seems Aisha is wrong. Sometimes it is right to kill. But is this the only sort of exception?

Notice that Carol's case involves killing a bad person so that innocent lives might be saved. But what about killing an *innocent* person to save innocent lives? Is *that* ever morally the right thing to do?

That's the question that we are going to examine in the rest of this chapter. Let's look at some different puzzle cases to see if we can figure out the answer.

The Grand Vizier's conundrum

The Grand Vizier was a humane and civilized advisor to the ruler of Moldania. One day, he was faced with a terrible decision. His country was invaded by the Warls, an awful, vicious race. They executed the ruler of Moldania and took the Grand Vizier to the City Square where they had lined up one hundred Moldanian children against a wall.

The Grand Vizier was presented with the following dilemma. He could shoot just one of the hundred children himself, and the others would then be set free. Or, if he refused, all one hundred children would be shot.

There were no other choices available to the Grand Vizier. For example, there was no possibility of the children being rescued. What should the Grand Vizier do?

On the one hand, the Grand Vizier could kill an innocent child. That would save the lives of 99 other children. The Grand Vizier knew that the Warls would be true to their word and release the 99 other children because he knew that this was something they always did on invading a country, and they had always been true to their word before.

On the other hand, the Grand Vizier could keep his hands clean and refuse to shoot an innocent child. But he knew the child would immediately be shot anyway, and so too would 99 others.

This is an awful decision for anyone to face.

Personally, I think I would kill one child in order to save the rest. I think that, on balance, that would be the best thing to do.

But if this is the correct decision, then it follows that killing an innocent person is sometimes the right thing to do.

What would you do, and why?

The submarine case

Here's another case. You are the head of a powerful country that possesses several nuclear-armed submarines. You know that one of these submarines has developed a mechanical fault that will shortly result in it launching all its nuclear missiles, killing millions of innocent people as a result.

You cannot contact the submarine's crew to prevent the launch. The only way to stop the catastrophe from happening is to destroy the sub, killing everyone on board.

What should you do?

It seems pretty clear to me that the right thing to do is to destroy the submarine, even though that would involve killing its entirely innocent and blameless crew. The alternative is just too awful to contemplate.

So it seems to me that sometimes the right thing to do is to kill innocent people if the result will be many more innocent lives saved.

The astronaut case

Here's a third example for you to think about.

The Spaceship Goliath has suffered a terrible accident, leaving only two crew members alive. The two astronauts, Sarah and Sade, are trapped in two different sections of the blasted hull. Sharon and Sade are rapidly running out of air. You have been despatched by Space Command to rescue the two astronauts and you arrive only minutes before Sarah and Sade will run out of air and suffocate.

Then you make a tragic discovery. You find that you can rescue only one of the two astronauts. For in order to rescue one of the astronauts, you will have to shut off the air supply to the other. You discover, in other words, that you can save one of the women only by killing the other.

What should you do?

Again, it seems pretty clear to me that the right thing to do in this case is to save one of the two lives, even though you can only do so by killing an innocent person. Surely it would be morally wrong to sit back and watch both women suffocate when one of them could be saved.

Calculating innocent lives saved

We have just looked at three cases in which it seems that the right thing to do is to kill an innocent person. That seems particularly clear in the last two cases. So it seems that sometimes it is OK to kill the innocent if the result will be innocent lives saved.

So, when faced with such decisions, is the right thing to do just to calculate what action will result in the most innocent lives saved, and then do that?

That sort of calculation would appear to give the right verdict in our first three cases. But what about the next case? Consider the Great Glugh's dilemma.

The Great Glugh's dilemma

The Great Glugh, ruler of Blastonia, was faced with a tough call. The chief of the Blastonian rescue services told the Great Glugh that a group of cavers was trapped after one of them, Ned, had became stuck in the exit hole. It wasn't Ned's fault: a rock had tumbled down and wedged him in.

The cave below Ned was flooding fast. Ned couldn't be safely removed without special equipment that was several hours away. But unless Ned was removed within the next half hour or so, the 20 other cavers trapped underneath Ned would all drown – though Ned himself would survive.

The chief of rescue services asked the Great Glugh what should be done. The 20 cavers could be saved, but only if the Great Glugh gave permission to kill Ned and cut his body out of the exit hole.

What should the Great Glugh's decision be?

In the first three cases, it seemed the right thing to do was to take an innocent life in order that other lives might be saved. If the right thing to do when presented with this sort of dilemma is simply to calculate which course of action will result in the greatest number of innocent lives saved, then obviously the right thing for the Great Glugh to do in this case is to kill Ned and save the other cavers.

But *is* that the right thing to do? I am not so sure.
What do you think?

The transplant case

Here's a case in which it seems pretty clear to me that it would
be quite *wrong* to kill an innocent person in order to save an
innocent life.

We are the doctors in charge of two patients. Tim, one of the
patients, has brain disease. He will be dead within a week or so.

The other patient, Jim, has heart failure. He will certainly die
within a few hours unless he receives a heart transplant.

Unfortunately, no transplant donor has been found.
But then we happen to notice that Tim has exactly the same
tissue type as Jim. So Tim's heart could be safely transplanted
into Jim and Jim would almost certainly survive.

What is the right thing to do? If we wait for Tim to die
before we take his heart it will be too late. Both men will die.
The only way to save Jim is by killing Tim.

But Tim isn't happy about being killed before his time is up.
He wants to spend his last week with his family.

What should we do?

Of course, we could kill Tim anyway. We could do it secretly
and painlessly. We could do it at night while Tim is sleeping.
Neither Tim nor his family need be any the wiser. His family

would just think Tim had died from brain disease a little earlier than expected. It's clear that if, when faced with these life-and-death situations, the right thing to do is always to do whatever will save the most innocent lives, then obviously the right thing to do in this case is to save Jim by killing Tim.

But is that the right thing to do?

Pretty obviously not! Almost everyone agrees that it would be morally very wrong indeed to kill Tim, even if the result would be that Jim survives.

Tim's 'right to life'

But *why* would it be wrong to kill Tim?

Some people would say: because human beings have rights. In particular, they have a *right to life*, a right not to be killed. True, a life might be saved by killing Tim. But it's wrong deliberately to infringe someone's rights, especially their right to life.

That's why Tim shouldn't be killed.

TIM HAS A RIGHT TO LIFE. IT IS MORALLY WRONG TO INFRINGE IT, NO MATTER HOW GOOD OUR INTENTIONS.

A tricky puzzle

But hang on a minute. If we should *never* under *any* circumstances infringe an innocent person's right to life, then it follows that it's also wrong to destroy the submarine in the submarine case. Blowing up the submarine would certainly involve infringing the crew members' rights to life. Yet it seems pretty clear that in the submarine case we should kill the crew.

The same is true of the astronaut case. In fact the astronaut case is a lot like the transplant case. In both, we can save one of two people only by killing the other. If we do nothing, both will die. Yet in one situation – the astronaut case – it seems that we should kill, while in the other – the transplant case – it seems we shouldn't.

So what's the essential difference between the transplant and astronaut cases, the difference that explains why it is OK to kill in one case but not the other?

I guess that, like me, you feel it *wouldn't* be wrong to kill one of the two astronauts in order to save the other. And I also guess that, like me, you feel pretty sure it *would* be wrong to kill the brain-diseased patient to save the heart patient. But that puts us both in a very awkward position. If we feel it's OK to kill in one case but not the other, then it's up to us to *justify* treating the two cases differently. I'm not so sure I can do that. Can you?

The case of the conjoined twins

As I say, it seems to me that sometimes it is morally acceptable to take an innocent life and sometimes it isn't. But, as we have seen, it's very hard to explain why it is OK to kill the innocent in some cases but not others. You may have an explanation of your own.

Here's a final case for you to think about. This time, it's not a case that I have made up. It's a *real* life-and-death case. I shall leave you to decide what should be done, and why.

A couple of years ago two girls were born joined together at the chest. They were conjoined, like this:

One twin was called Mary, the other Jodie. Jodie was bright and alert, but Mary had only a rudimentary brain and depended for her blood supply on Jodie's heart.

The parents and doctors faced a terrible decision. Leave the two girls connected and both would die within a matter of months. Separate them, and Jodie would probably survive, though Mary would certainly die.

The doctors involved believed that they should operate to separate the two girls. That way, at least one girl might be saved. But the parents, devout Catholics, objected on religious grounds. They believed that the operation to separate the two girls shouldn't go ahead, for it would involve killing one of the two girls. And that, they felt, would be wrong. Of course, they knew that the result of not killing Mary would be that *both* children would shortly die.

The doctors went to court and obtained permission to operate against the parents' wishes. Mary was killed. But Jodie survived.

But *was* that the right thing to do? Is this like the astronaut case, in which we thought it right to kill one innocent person in order to save the other? Or is it more like the transplant case, where we agreed that it would be wrong to kill one patient in order to save the other?

What do you think, and why?

Chapter 3

Does Murderous Mick deserve to be punished?

Here's Murderous Mick. He's just been captured trying to rob a bank. Mick shot a bank guard in the back, just for fun.

Obviously we think very badly of people like Murderous Mick. We hold them responsible for their dishonest, selfish and cruel behaviour. We believe that they deserve punishment. Mick will end up locked up in jail for years.

I guess you think, 'And quite right too. That's what Mick deserves.'

A 'common sense' view

That people who rob and murder deserve to be punished for what they do is, of course, the 'common sense' view. But is 'common sense' correct about this?

THAT'S RIGHT. I'M BLAMELESS!

As we will soon discover, there's a famous philosophical argument that *seems* to show that we are mistaken: Murderous Mick doesn't deserve punishment. In fact he's entirely blameless!

But before we get to that famous argument, let's quickly look at an obvious exception to the rule that people deserve to be punished for the harm they cause.

Mr Black gets shoved out of the window

We don't always hold people responsible for what they do. Suppose Mr Black gets pushed backwards out of a window. He lands on top of Mr Brown.

Mr Black's OK. But unfortunately, by landing on Mr Brown, Mr Black breaks Mr Brown's arm.

Is what happened Mr Black's fault? Does he deserve to be punished?

Surely not. Murderous Mick might deserve punishment, but not Mr Black. Why is this? After all, like Murderous Mick, Mr Black caused a serious injury.

The answer, it seems, is that Mr Black had *no control* over what happened. He was quite unable to stop himself being pushed out of the window or falling on Mr Brown.

How can it be Mr Black's fault that Mr Brown ended up with a broken arm? Surely we can only hold someone responsible for doing something they actually had some control over.

But, as I say, we *do* suppose that Murderous Mick deserves punishment. We suppose that, unlike Mr Black, Mick didn't have to do what he did. Instead of going in for bank robbing, murder and mayhem, Mick could have chosen to do good things with his life. Mick deserves punishment because, unlike Mr Black, he was *free to do otherwise*.

That, at least, is the 'common sense' view.

An extraordinary argument

Let's now turn to the famous philosophical argument I mentioned earlier. The argument is extraordinary because it seems to show that no one can ever be held responsible for what they've done.

Not even Murderous Mick!

Your first reaction to this is probably to say, 'Are you nuts? Of course Mick deserves punishment!' But don't make up your mind just yet. Let's take a closer look at the argument first. I call it, for obvious reasons, the *we-never-deserve-punishment argument*. I'll break the argument down into three parts.

The we-never-deserve-punishment argument. Part one: laws of nature

The argument begins with a scientific discovery. The universe, it seems, is everywhere ruled by *laws*. These laws of nature, as they are known, govern everything that happens physically. You might think of the laws of nature as a list of instructions that everything in the universe is compelled to obey, down to the very last atom.

For example, there's a law that governs how bodies attract each other gravitationally. Take the two planets Earth and Venus. These two objects exert a gravitational pull on each other. And there is a law of nature that says exactly how much pull these objects will exert on each other. The amount of pull depends on how massive the objects are and how close they are together. Big objects close together exert a strong pull.

Little objects far apart exert a weak pull.

Every pair of physical objects in the entire universe, from the tiniest pebble on the beach to a whole galaxy, must obey this law. There are no exceptions.

There are many other laws of nature, of course. In fact *everything that physically happens in the universe is governed by such laws.* This means that, if you know exactly how the universe is set up at any particular moment in time, down to the movement of the very last atom, and if you know all the laws of nature, then it is possible in principle for you to work out what will happen next, down to the movement of the very last atom.

It's as if the universe is a train and the laws of nature are its rails. If you know how fast the train is moving, and you know how the rails are laid, then you can predict exactly where the train will be at any point in the future. The train has no choice

about where it will end up. It's compelled to travel in a
particular direction by the rails. The same is true of the physical
universe. Every piece of physical matter is in the vice-like grip of
the same rigid laws. It's impossible for anything to happen other
than what actually happens. Earthquakes, volcanoes, rockfalls,
the tides, ice ages: everything that goes on physically is made to
happen, and could in principle have been predicted long
beforehand.

Philosophers have a name for the view that everything that
physically happens in the universe is determined by laws. It's
called *determinism*.

The we-never-deserve-punishment argument. Part two: we're nature's puppets

Which brings me to part two of the we-never-deserve-
punishment argument. We are physical beings ourselves. We have

physical bodies. But then it follows that our bodies are in the grip of the same physical laws as everything else:

What does this mean? Well, if we are also in the grip of these laws, then it seems *we are not free to do anything other than what we actually do*. For example, I just scratched the top of my head. But if determinism is true, I was no more able not to scratch my head than a pebble is free to float in mid-air or water is able to flow up hill unaided. Everything I do is physically determined, and could in principle have been predicted long before I decided to do it.

So I *am not free*. As physical beings, we are nature's puppets, dancing on her strings.

'But there are no laws of human nature...'

Before we get to part three of the we-never-deserve-punishment argument, let's quickly deal with a worry you might have about part two.

'Surely,' you may say, 'there are no laws governing *human behaviour*, are there? For example, there's no law that says that when someone is hungry and they know that there's food in the fridge, they will go to the fridge.'

Suppose Mary is hungry and she knows the only food is in the refrigerator.

Now, knowing human behaviour as I do, I can say that it's *pretty likely* that Mary will go to the fridge fairly soon. But there's no guarantee that she will. Perhaps Mary's on a diet. Or perhaps she's saving the food in the fridge for a party she's planning to have that evening.

The most I can say is that Mary will *probably* go to the fridge. There's no law compelling her to go to the fridge. She's free either to go or not to go.

Is this a good objection to the claim that we aren't free?

I don't think so.

True, there are no laws of human behaviour. But even if there are no laws of human behaviour, does it follow that Mary is free?

No, it doesn't follow. I admit there's no law that says that a hungry person who knows there is food in the fridge will go to the fridge. But a human being is a storm of tiny particles.

A HUMAN BEING IS A STORM OF TINY PARTICLES.

Mary is made out of molecules that are made out of atoms that are made out of electrons, protons and neutrons which are made out of still tinier particles all whizzing around. Each and every one of these particles is in the grip of the laws of nature. They cannot do anything other than what they do in fact do. Now it's *the laws governing these particles* that determine how Mary will behave. It is these laws that compel her to do whatever she does in fact do.

So Mary is not free. There may not be laws of human behaviour. It doesn't follow that what we do isn't determined by laws.

We human beings think we're free. But we're not really free. Our freedom is an illusion. We're nature's puppets.

The we-never-deserve-punishment argument. Part three: we're not to blame

Now we reach the final part of the we-never-deserve-punishment argument. If *none* of us is *ever* free – if we are unable to do anything other than what we in fact do – then how can we ever be held responsible for what we do? How can we ever deserve punishment?

After all, we said about Mr Black that he didn't deserve to be punished for landing on Mr Brown. That was because he had no control over what happened. He was compelled to land on top of poor Mr Brown.

But if determinism is true, the same is true of what Murderous Mick did. Murderous Mick was no more able not to shoot that poor bank clerk than Mr Black was able not to land on top of Mr Brown. Neither was free to do anything other than what they did do. But then neither deserves blame or punishment, surely?

True, the 'common sense' view is that someone like Murderous Mick deserves both blame and punishment. But it seems that 'common sense' is just wrong about this.

Philosophy v. 'common sense'

This is a fantastic conclusion, of course. In fact, like me, you probably can't make yourself believe the conclusion is true.

Still, is it rational to carry on believing that we are free and that we do sometimes deserve punishment? Am I justified in believing these things?

It seems I'm not. The we-never-deserve-punishment argument does appear to show that no one is free, and that no one ever deserves to be punished.

In philosophy you often come across arguments that contradict 'common sense'. One of the most fascinating, and sometimes infuriating, things about philosophy is the way it can challenge what we normally just take for granted.

Common sense has been wrong before, of course. It was once the 'common sense' view that the Earth is stationary. Almost everyone thought it 'just obvious' that the sun went round the Earth, not the other way round. But of course, all these people were mistaken. Science showed 'common sense' to be wrong.

Perhaps, by showing that everything that happens physically is determined, science has also shown that 'common sense' is wrong about us being free.

Sometimes, when 'common sense' views are challenged, people get very cross. That happened when scientists first showed that the Earth moves. They would shout 'That's just ridiculous! Of *course* the Earth doesn't move. You're just being *stupid!*' And they would stomp off in a huff.

I suppose that reaction is understandable. No one much likes having their most basic and fundamental beliefs challenged. It can be very uncomfortable to have someone come along and pick holes in what you have always taken for granted.

Still, the fact is that the really 'stupid' people were those who blindly stuck with 'common sense' even after they had been presented with overwhelming evidence that the Earth does move.

The same is true of someone who simply dismisses as stupid the conclusion that we're not free just because it's contrary to 'common sense'.

Where do we go from here?

So we have a puzzle – a very famous puzzle – that many philosophers have struggled with down the years.

On the one hand, we all believe that we are free. For example, I think I am free, right now, to do something different: to make a cup of tea, jump up and down on the spot, or shout 'Bananas!' out of the window.

But, on the other hand, we have seen an argument that appears to show that we're all completely mistaken about being free! I am no more able to do something different than water is free to flow uphill. We are, in truth, Nature's puppets, dangling helplessly on strings!

But if we aren't free, it seems, shockingly, that no one ever deserves punishment. Not even Murderous Mick!

All over the world, philosophers are struggling with this difficult puzzle. Are we free? Or aren't we? What's the answer? What do *you* think?

Faced with such an apparently devastating philosophical argument, defenders of the 'common sense' view that we are free have only one option. They must show that there is something wrong with the argument.

But if there *is* something wrong with the we-never-deserve-punishment argument, then *what* is wrong with it?

What do *you* think?

Meet the Fates

Before we try to figure out what, if anything, is wrong with the we-never-deserve-punishment argument, let's have a quick look at another, slightly different version of the view that we aren't free.

THE FATES

The Ancient Greeks believed in the Fates.

The Fates are beings who lay out the course of your life, giving you no option about how things turn out. For example,

if the Fates say you will be injured by a car next Wednesday, then you will. Try to avoid being injured if you want. But it will do no good. You can even stay in bed all day.

Somehow or other, the Fates will get you.

Those who believe in this sort of fate are called *fatalists*. Fatalists believe that there is no point in trying to prevent things from happening. For example, a fatalist might say, 'There's no point wearing a seatbelt: if I'm going to die in a car crash then I am going to die in a car crash – there's nothing I can do about it. What will be will be.'

Now the reason I mention fatalism is that it's very important not to muddle it up with determinism. Fatalism says that *our actions can have no effect*. Do what you like: things will still turn out the same way. Determinism, on the other hand, doesn't deny that our actions can make a difference to how things turn out. It just denies that we can act other than how we do.

There's no reason to suppose that fatalism is true. The Ancient Greeks might have believed in fate, but there's no evidence that our actions will have no effect on how things turn out. Quite the contrary, in fact. Wearing a seatbelt really can save your life.

But it *does* seem as if determinism is true. Science has revealed that the physical universe is governed by laws. And, being part of the physical universe, these laws apply to us as well. So we cannot do other than what we do.

Having clarified the difference between determinism and fatalism, let's take a closer look at the we-never-deserve-punishment argument.

Tom's 'proof' that he is free

Tom and Carol are sitting in The Magic Café here in Oxford. They often discuss philosophical puzzles over lunch and today they are talking about free will.

Carol has just explained the we-never-deserve-punishment argument to Tom. But Tom is totally unconvinced. He points to Carol's plate of vegetarian lasagne.

Tom: So you think that, even if I were to take your lunch, place it on the floor, and jump up and down on it, I would be entirely innocent and blameless? You think I would deserve not even one ounce of condemnation?

Carol looks up from her plate a little nervously.

Carol: Er, yes. You're not going to, are you?

Tom: No. But what if I did? I can't *really* believe you would think me blameless.

Carol: Well, I would probably feel very cross. I admit that. But then I feel cross when my computer crashes or when my car won't start. That doesn't mean that I think my computer and car deserve blame and punishment for not working, does it? That doesn't show that I believe they have free will.

Tom: No, I guess not. But still, it's obvious to me that I *am* free. I can *prove* it.

Carol: OK, go ahead and prove it.

Tom: Very well. Right now, I am free either to raise my arm or not raise my arm.

Tom sits motionless for a moment, and then suddenly raises his arm.

70

Tom: There, I raised my arm. But I was free not to raise it. I could have done either. So you see I *am* free. I am *not* nature's puppet.

Has Tom really proved that he is free? No, as Carol now explains.

Carol's water argument

Carol: You may *feel* free. But that doesn't guarantee that you *are* free. True, you may not *know* about the laws that compel you to behave as you do. But just because you don't know about them doesn't mean that they aren't there. They *are* there. That's precisely what science has shown.

Tom: But look, sometimes I raise my arm and other times I don't. So you see: I'm free to do either.

Carol: But the fact that you sometimes raise your arm and sometimes don't doesn't show that you are free.

Carol points to the water in her glass.

Carol: Look, sometimes water lies still like this. But sometimes it runs quickly in streams.

Sometimes it falls as rain or hangs in the air as a cloud. Does the fact that water behaves in these different ways on different occasions show that water is not governed by natural laws?

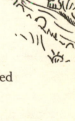

Tom: No. I guess not.

Carol: Right. So there you are, then. The fact that *you* behave in lots of different ways doesn't show that *you* aren't in the grip of the same laws.

Tom scratches the back of his neck. It still seems to him that, unlike the water in the glass, he is free to do his own thing.

Tom: But water behaves differently only because the circumstances in which you find it are different. Liquid water sometimes flows and sometimes doesn't, but that's because sometimes it's on a slope and sometimes not. Water will always behave exactly the same way if the circumstances are exactly the same.

Carol: That's true.

Tom: But I *don't* always behave in the same way, even when the circumstances *are* exactly the same. Yesterday we came into the Magic Café and I ordered soup. Today I ordered salad. Yet the circumstances today are just the same as they were yesterday. So you see – I am free in a way that the water in that glass is not.

Carol: No, you aren't. There are subtle differences between how you are today and how you were yesterday. Your internal make-up is different today. Your brain chemistry is subtly different, for example. Different patterns of neurons are firing. There are *all sorts* of differences. It's these differences that explain why you behave differently today, that explain why you made a different choice. If the situation today really were *absolutely* identical to the situation yesterday, right down to the very last atom, then you *would* have chosen soup today as well.

It seems Carol is right. It might seem obvious to you that you're free. But on closer examination it's not so obvious after all. In fact we still haven't spotted anything wrong with the argument that we're all nature's puppets.

The freedom of the soul
But Tom doesn't give up easily.

Tom: I still believe I'm free. It seems to me that you have a much too narrow, scientific view of the universe. Yes, science is powerful. But there is more to we humans than science can ever explain.

Carol: What do you mean?

Tom: I mean that each of us has a soul.

Carol: A soul?

Tom: Yes. Your soul is your *conscious mind*, that part of you that makes choices and decisions.

Carol: I see.

Tom: It is something outside the natural order. It's not part of the physical universe at all.

Carol: It's a non-physical thing?

Tom: That's right. It's even capable of existing on its own, without *any* physical body.

Many religious people believe in the existence of souls, of course. They believe that the death of the physical body does not mean the end of the person. What's essential to the person – their soul – can carry on. It is the soul that many Christians believe goes up to heaven after we die.

On Carol's view, people are physical things. They are not separate from their bodies.

But according to Tom, a person has a soul. The soul is something separate, something *non-physical*.

But what have souls to do with free will? Tom explains.

Tom: Being non-physical, the soul is not controlled by physical laws. Being apart from the physical world means it can do its own thing. So it *is* free.

This is an ingenious suggestion. Has Tom explained how we can be free after all?

A problem with the soul theory

Carol: But you haven't given me any r*eason* to suppose that souls exist, have you?

Tom: Well, I suppose not. Not yet.

Carol: And in any case, even if souls *do* exist, they s*till wouldn't allow us to act freely.*

Tom: Why not?

Carol: Because our bodies *are* physical. So they *are* in the grip of the laws of nature. What *they* do is determined in advance by how things are physically. But that means our bodies *still* can't do anything other than what they do, in fact, do.

Tom raises an eyebrow.

Tom: I'm not sure I follow.

Carol: Well, let's suppose you are right and I am a non-physical soul. According to you, I'm free to decide either to take a bite of that cake or to take a sip of that water. I decide to take a sip of water. But if determinism is true, what happens to my body is already fixed by the laws of nature. If the laws of nature say that my arm will reach out and grab the cake, then it will, whatever *I* might happen to decide.

So you see, even if we *do* have souls and they *are* free, that *still* wouldn't give us any control over what our bodies did.

Tom: Oh. I see.

Carol: In fact, if we had souls, they would be disconnected from our bodies, unable to have *any* effect on what they did. So, as we clearly *can* affect what our bodies do, it follows that *we don't have souls.*

This is an interesting line of argument. If determinism is true, it really would seem to follow that we don't have souls.

Is the brain an exception to the laws of nature?

But Tom is unpersuaded by Carol's argument.

Tom: You're simply assuming that what your body does is fixed by the laws of nature plus how things are physically. But *that's not true.* Your soul can come in and affect what's going on physically.

Carol: How does it do that?

Tom: It's as if the soul and the brain are equipped with little transmitters and receivers.

SOUL

BRAIN

When I decide I want to raise my arm, my soul transmits a signal to my brain. That causes something to happen in my brain, which in turn causes electrical signals to be sent to my arm. That raises my arm.

Carol: But that's *ridiculous*! That would mean that something happening in your brain has no *physical* cause. Being caused by the signal sent from something non-physical – your soul – it would not be physically determined.

Tom: Exactly.

Carol: But *every* physical event has a physical cause. That's a law of nature.

Tom: Yes, generally speaking, physical events have physical causes. But there's an exception to the rule: the human brain. Some things happen in the brain that *don't* have a physical cause. Some of what goes on in the brain is caused by *the soul* – something *non-physical*.

Carol: So the laws of nature apply throughout the entire universe, with one exception: the human brain?

Tom: Yes.

Carol: What a load of unscientific tosh!

Tom's explanation of how the soul and the body interact is certainly a lot to swallow. The suggestion that the laws of nature apply throughout the entire universe *except for one place*, the human brain, is pretty implausible. Why suppose that the laws of nature make an exception of the human brain?

Why it may still be right to punish Mick

Up to now, we haven't spotted anything wrong with the we-never-deserve-to-be-punished argument.

So let's suppose, for the sake of argument, that it's true that we can't act freely and so never deserve punishment. Does it

I'M BLAMELESS! SO YES, YOU SHOULD RELEASE ME!

then follow that it is a mistake to punish murderous Mick for what he did? Should we release him?

Actually, it doesn't follow. Even if Murderous Mick doesn't deserve punishment, there are still good reasons why we should send him to prison. Here are three:

First, punishment may have a *deterrent* effect. Even if we can't act freely — even if we are physically determined — our behaviour can still be altered. And it might be altered by the threat of punishment. People may be *caused* to act differently if they think they will go to prison. If we punish people for committing crimes, then people may be less likely to commit those crimes. If so, then here is a good reason for punishing criminals anyway, whether or not they deserve it.

Second, by sending a criminal to prison we may be able to help them. Some prisons aim to *rehabilitate* prisoners, so that they are less likely to offend again. Again, even if we are not free, rehabilitation may *cause* us to act differently.

Third, by locking murderers like Mick up, we can *prevent* them from murdering again.

SEE — THERE ARE STILL GOOD REASONS WHY WE SHOULD LOCK YOU UP.

OH DEAR.

So there are still good reasons why we should lock Murderous Mick up: deterrence, rehabilitation and prevention. Of course, none of this is to say that Mick deserves to be locked up. It's just that it seems to be a good idea to lock him up anyway, whether or not he deserves it.

The puzzle

In this chapter, we have looked at a famous philosophical puzzle: the puzzle is raised by the we-never-deserve-to-be-punished argument. Philosophers call it the *puzzle of free will*.

Philosophers have been struggling with the puzzle for hundreds of years. Even today, at universities across the world, philosophers and scientists are still trying to solve it.

The puzzle is this: it seems that, if determinism is true, then we can't act freely. But then it appears that none of us ever deserves punishment for what we do.

Yet this is *absurd*, isn't it? *Of course* we can act freely. *Of course* we sometimes deserve to be punished for what we have done. Don't we?

What do you think?

Chapter 4

Where did the universe come from?

Readers of The Philosophy Files *will be familiar with the first argument in this chapter. But this chapter also contains many important new arguments, including the levers-of-the-universe argument, the simplicity argument, the lottery fallacy and two new arguments about faith. So do keep reading!*

The Big Bang

Sometime between eight and twenty billion years ago something utterly astonishing happened. The universe *began*.

THE BIG BANG.

It started with the *Big Bang*: a colossal explosion in which matter, space and even time itself came into being.

When you look up at the night sky, what you see is the debris left by this extraordinary event. The countless stars, planets and galaxies are the smoky entrails of that huge, unimaginably violent moment of creation.

We know that the Big Bang happened. But *why* did it happen?

Why does the universe exist? Or, to put it another way, why is there *something* rather than *nothing*?

This is a question with which mankind has been struggling for thousands of years. It is, perhaps, the greatest mystery of all.

God

One of the most popular answers to the question about the origin of the universe is that it was created by God. That is the answer that we are going to look at in this chapter.

What is God like?

If God did create the universe, then what is He like?

According to Jews, Christians and Muslims, God has at least three characteristics.

First of all, God is *all-powerful*. That means He can do anything. God can flatten mountains and part seas.

81

He can bring the dead back to life. God could even destroy the
entire universe at a moment's notice if He chose to.

Second, God is all-knowing. There's
nothing God is unaware of. He
knows all our secrets and
innermost thoughts. You can't
hide anything from God.

Third, God is all-good.
God loves us and cares for
us as if we were His
children.

Other gods

Of course, not all religions think of God
in this way. One religion – Buddhism – has no god at all.
Others, such as Hinduism and the religions of the Ancient
Egyptians, Greeks and Romans, have many.

And not all religions think of the supernatural being or
beings that rule over us as being particularly pleasant. The gods
of the Ancient Greeks, for example, could be uncaring and
sometimes rather cruel towards us mortals.

A COUPLE OF GREEK GODS

But that's not true of the God of Jews, Christians and Muslims. Their God, if He exists, would never be cold or callous.

It's the claim that there is such an all-powerful, all-knowing and all-good God that we are going to look at in this chapter.

Is belief in God justified?

Very many people believe in God. For some, belief in God is a matter of faith. They insist you should just *believe*. It doesn't matter whether or not there are good grounds for believing. But as philosophers, we want to know what it's *reasonable* to believe. We want to know if there is good *evidence* of His existence. Is there a sound *argument* for the existence of God?

We are going to look at three of the very best arguments for God's existence. We will also be looking at one famous argument that *seems* to show that there is no God.

Our job will be to think like detectives. We're going to take a cool, careful look at the arguments and the evidence and try to figure out, as best we can, what is most likely to be true.

Let's start with the first argument for the existence of God. I call it *the cause argument*.

Argument one: the cause argument

Aisha has spent the weekend in France with her friend Tom, and now they are travelling back to England on the ferry. They are out on deck, lying on their sun-loungers and sipping tea as the ferry glides peacefully through the night.

It's cold, and the stars are twinkling brightly. Over to the right, a few streaks of cloud are bathed by the last pink glow of sun. To the left, a full moon is beginning to peek over the horizon. Ahead of them, to the south, they can just make out some lights on the French coast.

Tom takes another mouthful of tea and places his cup carefully on the table between them.

Suddenly, there's a faint whoosh, followed by an explosion of light over to the south.

A ship has launched a flare.

Tom watches as the flare

drifts slowly downwards, bathing the horizon with its eerie green light. Then Tom picks up his cup and starts to speak.

Tom: You know, the more I think about it, the more certain I become that there just *must* be a God.

Aisha: What makes you so certain?

Tom waves his cup up at the stars.

Tom: How else do we explain the existence of *all this*? Where did it all *come from*?

Aisha: Come from?

Tom: Yes. Several billion years ago the universe began. There was a Big Bang.

Aisha: I know.

Tom: Now, what I want you to explain to me is *why* the Big Bang happened. Why, out of nothing at all, did a universe suddenly appear?

Aisha: Couldn't it just pop into existence for no reason?

Tom: Don't be ridiculous. Things don't *just happen*, do they? There's *always* a cause. Avalanches, earthquakes, bridge collapses, stock market crashes – we suppose they *all* have causes, even if we don't always happen to know what the cause is.

He points to the dying light of the flare.

Tom: Take that explosion just now. No one would think that explosion happened *for no reason*, would they? Explosions don't *just happen*, do they? It's reasonable to suppose the explosion had a cause, even if we don't know what it was. Correct?

Aisha: Yes. It's reasonable to suppose someone caused the flare to
explode. By lighting its fuse, I imagine.

Tom: Right. But if it's reasonable to suppose that *that* explosion had a
cause, then it's reasonable to suppose the Big Bang had a cause too,
isn't it?

Tom takes a final swig of tea and beams triumphantly.

Tom: So there you are! *God must exist*! If the
Big Bang had a cause, then *God
must exist as its cause*!

Aisha: God lit the fuse?

Tom: Precisely!

What do you think of Tom's
first argument?

It does look pretty convincing.
Certainly, very many people take the cause
argument to show that belief in God is at least pretty reasonable.

A problem with the cause argument

But Aisha isn't persuaded. She thinks she's spotted a fatal flaw in
Tom's argument.

Aisha: There's a problem with your argument, Tom. You begin
with the claim that *everything* has a cause, right?

Tom: Yes.

Aisha: But if *everything* has a cause, then it follows that *God* has
a cause, doesn't it?

Tom: I suppose it does.

Aisha: So what I want to know is: if *everything* has a cause, then
what caused God to exist?

Aisha's question is a good one. Suppose God did cause the universe.

The problem with Tom's argument is that, if it establishes that God must exist as the cause of the universe, then it also establishes the existence of something else: a cause of God.

But of course, if *everything* has a cause, then whatever caused God to exist must have a cause.

And that too must have a cause. And so on without end!

You can see that, if absolutely *everything* has a cause, then there's going to be an *endless chain* of causes leading up to the creation of the universe. God would merely be the last link in the chain.

And of course, hardly anyone who believes in God is prepared to accept *that*.

God is the exception to the rule

The sea breeze ruffles Tom's hair. He stares for a moment or two at the tea leaves lining the bottom of his now empty cup. And then he has an idea.

Tom: Ah. I see. What I *should* have said, of course, is that everything has a cause *except for God*. God is the exception to the rule.

Aisha: Exception to the rule?

Tom: Yes. He is the one thing that doesn't need a cause. So you see, as everything except God needs a cause, it follows that God must exist as the cause of the universe. But as God is the exception to the rule that everything has a cause, we don't then have to introduce a cause for God.

Notice that by altering his argument very slightly − by saying, not that *everything* has a cause, but that *everything except God* has a cause − Tom has managed to avoid introducing an endless chain of causes.

Why make God the exception?

Aisha is impressed by Tom's new, improved version of the cause argument. But she's still not convinced.

Aisha: A clever move. But I'm afraid your argument still doesn't work.

Tom: Why not?

Aisha: Well, if you're going to start making exceptions to the rule that everything has a cause, why make God the exception? Why not just say that *the universe* is the exception, instead?

Tom: Well, I guess you *could* say that.

Aisha: Then we wouldn't need to introduce God as the cause of the
universe, would we?

Tom: I suppose not.

Aisha: So you see, unless you can come up with some reason why I
should think God and not the universe is the exception to the rule,
you haven't given me any reason to believe that God exists.

Is this a good criticism of Tom's argument?

The endless tower of animals

Tom scrunches his face up the way he does when
he's not really sure about something. So Aisha tries
to explain her criticism in a different way.

She picks up a pencil and starts to sketch out this
drawing on a napkin.

Aisha: Did you know that in Hindu mythology the Earth is supposed to
sit on the back of a great turtle, like this?

Tom: Why believe that?

Aisha: Well, I guess the ancient Hindus wanted to explain how
everything is held up. *Everything* falls unless there is something to
hold it up. Apples, chairs, rocks: they all tumble without support. But
that raises the question: *why doesn't the Earth itself fall?*

Aisha points to her sketch.

Aisha: This would be their explanation: it's held up by a *big elephant.*

Tom: Weird.

Aisha: Now there's something pretty unsatisfactory about this elephant
explanation, isn't there?

Tom: You mean, it just invites the question, 'And what holds the elephant
up?'

Aisha: Exactly. And do you know how they answered that question?
Tom: No.
Aisha: They said that the elephant is held up by a big turtle.

Aisha draws a turtle under the elephant, like this:
Tom points to the turtle.

Tom: But then what holds the turtle up?
Aisha: Good question! In fact the Hindus just stopped
at the turtle. But *why stop there?* Surely the turtle
will need another animal to hold it up, and the
animal that holds the turtle up will need yet another animal to hold
it up, and so on without end.
Tom: But then there would be an *endless tower of
animals*!
Aisha: Exactly! And if they are going to stop at *one*
of the animals – the turtle – and say *this* animal
doesn't need anything to hold it up – if they are
going to say that this animal is *the exception to
the rule* that everything needs holding up –then
why not make the Earth the exception to the rule
instead? What's the justification for introducing *any animals at all?*

Tom gazes out to sea.

Tom: There isn't any.
Aisha: Correct! So you see, by introducing these giant animals, the
ancient Hindus never *really* solved the mystery of why everything
doesn't fall. They just pushed it back a step.
Tom: That's true.
Aisha: Now I think exactly the same is true of *your* explanation of why
there is something rather than nothing. You suppose that God

solves that mystery: He created everything. But God doesn't *really* solve the mystery. Just like the big elephant theory, you have merely pushed the problem back a step. For God's existence then needs to be explained, doesn't it?

I think Aisha is correct. As it stands, Tom's justification for believing in God involves the same sort of mistake as the justification for believing in the giant elephant and the giant turtle. Neither argument gives us *any reason at all* to suppose that these fantastic beings exist.

A profound mystery
Still, Aisha is quite prepared to admit that there is a mystery about where the universe came from.

Tom: So *where did* the universe come from, then, if not from God? How do *you* explain its existence?

Aisha: To be honest, I can't. I am merely pointing out that you haven't given me the slightest reason to suppose that it was created by God.

Tom: Hmm.

Aisha: In fact, *whatever* you might point to as the explanation for why there's something rather than nothing – be it God or some other thing: the great banana being, for example – just becomes one more part of the 'something' that then needs explaining.

Tom: I suppose that's true. So the mystery can *never* be solved?

Aisha: Precisely. So you see, I'm quite prepared to admit that there *is* a deep and profound mystery about why there's something rather than nothing. I just don't see how God helps solve it.

Argument two: the levers-of-the-universe argument
Tom lies back in his lounger and stares up at the stars. The moon is higher now and its light shimmers on the dancing waves.

Tom has to admit: as it stands, his cause argument has turned out to be a bit of a flop. Still, he feels quite sure that he can come up with a better argument, given a little time.

Tom pours himself some more tea.

Tom: Another cup? OK, here's a *much* better argument. We inhabit a universe governed by *laws*, don't we?

Aisha: You mean, the *laws of nature*?

Tom: Exactly. The laws that govern gravity and motion and so on. The laws that scientists investigate.

Aisha: I see.

Tom: Now, the universe could have been governed by quite *different* laws, couldn't it?

Aisha: In what way?

Tom: Well, take gravity for example. Gravity is a sort of pulling force that all physical objects exert on each other.

Tom pours some more tea into his cup.

Tom: Big objects like the Earth have a lot of gravity. Which is why we stick to it rather than float off into space. It's gravity that keeps us glued to the deck right now, and that's pulling the tea out of this teapot and into this cup.

Aisha: I know.

Tom: Now the laws governing gravity could have been different, couldn't they? Gravity *could* have been much stronger. Or much weaker.

Aisha: I suppose it could.

Tom: In fact, we can think of the universe as having levers that fix what the laws of nature are. The gravity lever is set at a particular position.

But it could have been set much higher…

… or much lower…

… couldn't it? In fact it could have been set so that there is no gravity at all.

Aisha: I guess so.

Tom: But scientists tell us that if the various laws of nature had been only a *little* bit different, life could never have evolved.

Aisha: Really?

Tom: Yes. For example, if gravity had been just a *bit* stronger, the universe would have lasted only a moment or two after the Big Bang before collapsing in on itself in a Big Pop. Or, if gravity had been just a *bit* weaker, stars and planets capable of supporting life would never have formed.

Aisha: I see.

Tom: Either way, *we would not be here.*

Tom appears to be right. Many scientists now believe that if the laws of nature had been only *slightly* different, then conscious beings such as ourselves could never have evolved.

Tom: Now, if the levers of the universe were set at *random*, the chances of hitting on a combination of positions that would produce conscious beings like us would be incredibly small.

Aisha: So you say.

Tom: Yet the levers *were* set that way, weren't they?

Aisha: Yes.

Tom: It's just too much of a coincidence that the levers are set like that. It's far more plausible that someone *deliberately* set the universe up this way. Someone must have *fine-tuned* the universe to produce us!

Aisha: And this someone was God?

Tom: It's *the only plausible explanation*!

Let's call Tom's new argument the *levers-of-the-universe argument*. Is it a good argument?

I must say, this is one of the best-looking arguments for the existence of God that I have come across. At first sight, the argument does look very persuasive indeed.

Are you convinced?

The lottery fallacy

Not everyone is persuaded by the levers-of-the-universe argument. One common criticism is that it involves the lottery fallacy. Aisha starts to explain the problem.

Aisha: That's an ingenious argument. But *still* no good, I'm afraid.
Tom: Why not?
Aisha: Look, suppose I enter a lottery. One million tickets are sold, of which I buy just one.

But then mine turns out to be the winning ticket. Now the chances of my winning were very small, correct?
Tom: Yes. A million to one against.
Aisha: Yet I did win. So here's my big question: *Is it likely that someone rigged the lottery in my favour?*

Tom thinks hard for a moment.

Tom: I don't think so.

Aisha: Why not?

Tom: Well, one of the million tickets had to win. And *whichever* ticket won would have had only a one-in-a-million chance of winning.

Aisha: Right. So the fact that *my* ticket had only a one-in-a-million chance of winning gives me no reason to suppose the lottery was rigged in my favour.

Tom: I agree.

Aisha smiles.

Aisha: But your levers-of-the-universe argument involves *exactly the same sort of mistake*!

Tom: Why?

Aisha: Well, the levers of the universe had to be set *some* way or other, didn't they? And each of the different ways the levers might have been set was equally likely, correct?

Tom: Yes.

Aisha: So the mere fact that it's very unlikely that they should just happen to be set *this* way, to produce us, gives us no grounds for supposing we have been anything other than lucky. There's no reason to suppose someone must have *deliberately* positioned the levers this way.

Tom scratches his head. He has to admit: Aisha does *appear* to be right. If it's a mistake to suppose someone deliberately rigged the lottery in the winner's favour, then surely it's a mistake to suppose that someone deliberately rigged the universe in our favour.

Tom: Hmm. *Maybe* you are right. *Perhaps* my argument does involve the same mistake.

Does Tom's levers-of-the-universe argument involve the lottery fallacy? I'll leave you to make up your own mind about that.

Argument three: the simplicity argument

Tom now comes up with his third and final argument for the existence of God. I call it the *simplicity argument*.

It takes Tom a couple of minutes to explain the argument. He starts by talking about *electrons*.

Tom: OK. Whether or not my levers-of-the-universe argument works, I think I *still* have one really good argument left.

Aisha: What is it?

Tom: Let's start by thinking about electrons.

Aisha: Electrons?

Tom: Yes. An electron is one of the tiny, whizzy particles scientists think atoms are made out of.

AN ATOM

Aisha: I know.

Tom: Now, *no one has ever seen an electron*, have they? Not even down a microscope. They are far smaller than anything we might observe.

Aisha: Of course.

Tom: But if no one has ever observed an electron, why do scientists suppose they exist?

Aisha furrows her brow and thinks hard for a moment or two.

Aisha: Well, there are things that we *can* observe that electrons explain. For example, they explain why lightning storms happen. And they explain why various chemical reactions occur.

This is all perfectly true. Electrons explain these and many other things too.

THIS LIGHTNING CAN BE EXPLAINED BY APPEALING TO ELECTRONS!

The gremlins theory

Tom continues with the next part of the simplicity argument.

Tom: But look, the mere fact that electrons, if they exist, would *explain* these things doesn't *by itself* give us much reason to suppose they exist.

Aisha: It doesn't?

Tom: No. After all, there are *all sorts* of invisible things that might explain why lightning storms, chemical reactions and so on happen, aren't there?

Aisha: Such as?

Tom: Well, we *could* appeal to tiny invisible *gremlins*, couldn't we?

We could say that these gremlins like big flashes and bangs, so they go up into the sky to make storms.

A GREMLIN

WEEE! HE HE! WHOA!

And they dislike chaos and irregularity, which
is why they always make chemicals behave the
same way in test tubes.

Aisha: You're right. We *could* appeal to gremlins
instead of electrons. But that would be a
ridiculous explanation.

Tom: Why?

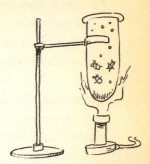

Aisha is correct. The gremlin theory is a
downright silly theory. But why?

Aisha thinks she has the answer.

Aisha: Because the gremlin theory is terrifically *complicated*: it involves
lots and lots of little beings with their own complex little minds, all
running around making things happen.

Tom: I agree. In fact, with their complex minds filled with their likes and
dislikes, *these gremlins are at least as complicated as what they're
supposed to explain.*

Aisha: Exactly.

Tom: The electron hypothesis, on the other hand, is *simple and elegant*.
It involves just a single sort of entity with a few very simple
properties. So while we're *not* justified in supposing gremlins exist,
we *are* justified in supposing electrons exist.

Tom and Aisha are right. It can be reasonable to suppose that
certain unobservable things exist if they provide the neatest,
simplest explanation for the complex order we find around us.

'If it's reasonable to believe in electrons, then it's reasonable to believe in God'

Tom sinks back in his lounger. He is about to reach the
punchline of the simplicity argument.

Tom: But if it's reasonable to believe in electrons, then it's reasonable to believe in God!

Aisha can't see what Tom is getting at.

Aisha: Why do you say that?

Tom takes another sip of tea, and starts to explain.

Tom: It's simple. The universe isn't just a random, chaotic mess, is it? It is full of order. It is full of rich patterns and regularities. It's governed by laws.

Aisha: True.

Tom: Now we can explain all this order and complexity by supposing that there is something invisible behind the scenes that accounts for the order we see around us. Something *very simple*.

Aisha: And what would this simple thing be?

Tom: God, of course. For *God is a very simple being.*

Aisha: He is?

Tom: Yes. He is a single entity with three simple properties: infinite power, infinite knowledge and infinite goodness. And yet, by supposing this single, simple entity exists, we can account for the complex order we see around us. It can all be explained as a result of God's grand design. God made the universe this way *for us*, so that we could evolve and develop and finally come to understand the universe and the God who created it for us.

So you see – I can give exactly the same justification for believing in God as you gave for believing in electrons! If you believe in electrons, then you should believe in God, too.

Is Tom correct? Can we justify belief in God in the same way we justify belief in electrons?

Aisha's criticism of the simplicity argument
Aisha doesn't think God can be quite as simple as Tom makes out.

Aisha: You claim that the theory that God created the universe gives a very simple explanation for the complex order we see around us?

Tom: I do.

Aisha: And God *designed* the universe?

Tom: That's right. Down to the very last detail.

Aisha: But if God designed the universe, then *all the order and complexity of the universe was present in God's mind before it was created.*

Tom: True.

Aisha: But that makes God at least as complex as what you are using Him to explain!

I think Aisha is right. True, the theory that God created the universe does *appear* simple and elegant. But only while we think of God as being just infinitely powerful, knowledgeable and good.

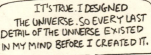

When we look more closely at the theory, it turns out that God must actually be highly complex. If every last feature of the universe was planned by God, then *all its complexity existed in God's mind before He created* it.

101

But then *God is at least as complex as His creation.*

So it looks as if the theory that God created the universe suffers from the same problem as the gremlins theory: God is no less complex than what He's supposed to explain. It seems we are left with no more reason to believe in God than we have to believe in gremlins.

An argument *against* the existence of God

So far, we have looked at three arguments for the existence of God. Aisha hasn't been persuaded by any of them.

Of course, even if it's true that there aren't any good arguments for the existence of God, that doesn't show that there's no God. Just because we can't show that something is true doesn't mean it *isn't* true.

But what if there is a good argument *against* the existence of God?

Aisha glances out at the gently churning sea. Then she looks down at the cup in her hands. The throb of the engines makes tiny waves form across the surface of the liquid. A tea leaf floats gently about like a little ship. Aisha idly prods at the leaf with her finger tip. Then she starts to speak.

Aisha: It seems to me you haven't really given me any reason to believe in God. And in fact there's very good reason to suppose there is no God.

Tom: What reason?

Aisha: Well, God is supposed by Christians, Jews and Muslims to be all-powerful and all-knowing, isn't He?

Tom: Of course.

Aisha: He is also supposed to be *all good*, isn't He?

Tom: Certainly. That's one of God's defining attributes. He loves and cares for us.

Aisha: But it's obvious that there's no such being!

Tom: Why obvious?

Aisha: Look around you. I admit that there's much that is wonderful about the world. Yes, God made 'all things bright and beautiful'.

But let's not forget that God also made earthquakes, famines, the Black Death and haemorrhoids.

The world is full of innocent children dying slow, agonizing deaths, apparently for no reason. Yet you claim the world was created by an all-powerful, all-knowing God *who loves and cares* for us?

Tom: Yes.

Aisha: So why does He torture children to death? Would you do that to *your* children?

Tom: Of course not.

Aisha: So why does God do it?

This is undoubtedly the most famous of all the arguments against the existence of God. It has been around for many hundreds of years. To this day, many of those who believe in God continue to struggle with the problem it raises. If God is all powerful, all-knowing and all-good, then why is there so much suffering in the world?

Some might suggest that God *can't* prevent our suffering. But of course that cannot be true. God is all powerful; He can do anything. He can stop our suffering. In fact, God could have made a world free of all pain and suffering if He wanted to. He could have made the Earth as heaven is meant to be.

Some might say that God doesn't *realize* we are suffering. But that can't be right either, can it? For God is all-knowing.

So it seems that God, if He exists, must *make us suffer on purpose*. But God is, by definition, all-good. He would never be deliberately cruel. He would never torture a child to death for no reason.

The inescapable conclusion would seem to be that *there is no God*. As Aisha explains, even if we can show the universe *was* designed by some sort of intelligent creator, it seems pretty clear this creator cannot be God, who, by definition, is all-powerful, all-knowing and all-good.

Aisha: It seems to me that, if there is an all-powerful and all-knowing creator, then He is some sort of evil sadist.

Either that or our creator *doesn't much care about us*. Maybe he's idly studying us. Maybe he is like a child, curious about what happens to ants if you burn them with a magnifying glass.

He's not *deliberately* cruel. He just doesn't much care.

Aisha appears to be correct. Even if we *did* have reason to believe the universe has a creator (which, if Aisha is right, is in any case very doubtful), there's no reason to suppose that this creator is at all *nice*, or even particularly interested in us humans. In fact it does seem, as Aisha says, that our creator couldn't care less.

Tom isn't convinced. He thinks there is a loving God watching over us. But then *why* does God cause all this suffering? *Why* does He choose to make children die in great pain? Tom isn't sure.

Tom: I agree that the sort of God I believe in would never inflict an agonizing death on a child for no reason. There must be *some* explanation, *some* reason behind it. We just don't know what that reason is.

The suffering is punishment

If Tom is right and there are good reasons for the suffering God causes us, then what might these reasons be?

Some believe the suffering is *punishment*. God is punishing us for our sins.

But this doesn't seem a very likely explanation. After all, babies haven't sinned, have they? So why does God punish them?

AS A PUNISHMENT FOR YOUR WRONGDOING, I CONDEMN YOUR TWO CHILDREN TO A HORRIBLE DISEASE.

Some believe the suffering of young children is punishment for the sins of the grown-ups.

But again, this doesn't really make much sense. How would we feel about a court that punished criminals by giving their children painful diseases?

We would be horrified! We would consider it *extremely* unfair. In fact we would think it downright immoral. Surely a good and loving God would never do such a despicable thing.

We cause the suffering

Others suggest that our suffering is not God's fault, but ours. It is *we* who cause wars and famines, for example, not God.

But this is unconvincing. For there is clearly a great deal of suffering in the world that *isn't* caused by us. Take childhood diseases, such as leukaemia. You might suggest that *some* cases of leukaemia are caused by us. For example, some people believe that certain cases of leukaemia are caused by pollution, which is our fault.

But it's clear that *most* cases of leukemia occur naturally. The same goes for other diseases and natural disasters, such as earthquakes. The suffering that these things create cannot be blamed on us. If God exists, they are His responsibility.

The suffering is to *improve* us

Some people have tried to defend belief in God by insisting that our suffering is designed to *improve* us. After all, suffering can be character building, can't it? Someone who has gone through a painful illness and come out of the other side may be strengthened by the experience. They may learn from the experience.

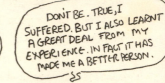

In order to allow us to develop into the virtuous people God wants us to be, God needed to put suffering in the world. Our suffering is, ultimately, all for the best.

Does this suggestion deal with the problem of suffering?

I don't see that it does. To begin with, you might wonder why God didn't just make us strong and virtuous right from the start. Why all the needless agony?

Even if suffering *is* the unavoidable price we must pay for virtue, it's difficult to understand why God dishes out suffering in the way He does. Why do mass-murdering dictators live out their lives in luxury? Why do lovely, generous people have horrendous diseases inflicted upon them?

It is, to say the least, hard to comprehend how the seemingly random distribution of suffering in the world could really be 'all for the best'.

God works in mysterious ways

Still, Tom insists that, while we can't see how our suffering is for
the best, still, it might be for the best.

Tom: Look, we can't be expected to understand *everything*, can we? God
works in mysterious ways. I'm sure the suffering we endure *is*
ultimately for the good. It's just that, being mere humans, we can't
see how.

Is this a good reply to the problem of suffering? Aisha certainly
doesn't think so.

Aisha: But that's just admitting defeat! You're pointing out that, despite
the fact that the suffering doesn't *seem* to make any sense at all,
nevertheless it *might* ultimately make sense. Well, yes, it *might*. But
that's not to deny that the evidence really does, on the face of it,
point very firmly towards there being no God.

Aisha does appear to be correct. Yes, it's possible that God exists.
Yes, our suffering *may* be all for the best. Aisha's point remains:
given the evidence, this seems very unlikely.

Aisha: After all, you can say about almost *any* belief, no matter how
silly, 'But it *might* be true.' There *might* be fairies at the bottom of
the garden. But the fact is the evidence strongly suggests otherwise.

Faith

If belief in God is unreasonable, does that matter? After all, many
of those who believe in God insist that reason has little to do
with their belief. They insist we must just *believe*, irrespective of
what the arguments or the evidence might suggest. Belief in
God is ultimately a matter of faith, not reason.

Let's finish by taking a closer look at this sort of religious faith.

Placing our faith in others

Some argue that, just as it's a good thing to place our faith in those around us, so it's also a good thing to place our faith in God. In fact, that's just what Tom thinks.

Tom: Look, even if there's little reason to suppose God exists, it is still a good thing to believe. Faith is life-enhancing!

Aisha: In what way?

Tom: Well, you agree, don't you, that it's good to place our faith in others? Take the captain of this ship, for example. We place our faith in him when we get on board. We trust he will act responsibly.

Aisha: True.

Tom: In fact we *have* to have faith in other people, in their trustworthiness and kindness, don't we? I trust my bank manager to look after my money. I trust my shopkeeper not to sell me rotten or poisoned food. I trust my friends to stand by me when I am in trouble. Without this sort of trust life would be difficult, if not impossible, wouldn't it?

Aisha: That's true, too. In a sense, *faith makes the world go round.*

Tom: So you see, placing our faith in others is a positive, life-enhancing thing to do. Indeed, we generally consider it an *admirable* thing, don't we?

Aisha: Generally speaking, yes we do.

Tom: But then *it must also be a positive, life-enhancing thing to place our faith in God.* Don't you agree?

Faith in Santa Claus: a bad side to faith?

Aisha shakes her head.

Aisha: I'm afraid I don't agree. Look, when we talk about 'placing our faith in others', we mean trusting in their good character, trusting that they will act kindly and responsibly. Right?

Tom: Yes.

Aisha: But *that* sort of faith simply takes for granted that the people in whom we place our trust *actually exist.* It's only admirable to place your trust in someone if you already have *pretty good reason* to suppose the person in question is really there. Otherwise it's downright silly.

Tom: Is it?

Aisha: Yes. Look, think about this case. Two children are looking forward to Christmas Day. But their parents are penniless. They can afford neither Christmas dinner nor gifts. But they don't want to disappoint their children. So what do they do?

Despite the fact that they have little reason to believe that Santa Claus exists, and plenty of reason to suppose he doesn't, these parents *place their faith in Santa* to deliver presents on  Christmas Day! Not only that, they encourage their children to believe in Santa too. 'Don't worry, kids', they say. 'Have faith in Santa. He's a good person. I am sure he will bring us presents on Christmas Day!' What would you think of such parents?

Tom: They are very foolish!

Aisha: Of course.

Tom: Worse than that, they have misled their poor children. These children are bound to be terribly upset and disappointed come Christmas Day when no presents turn up.

Aisha: I agree.

Tom: The parents' behaviour is *downright irresponsible*!

Aisha: Absolutely. But if I am right that there are no decent arguments for the existence of God and an extremely good argument against, *isn't it just as silly and irresponsible for religious people to encourage others to place their faith in God?*

Is Aisha right? If she is correct about the arguments (and that is a very big 'if', of course) is it as foolish to encourage others to believe in God as it is to encourage them to believe in Santa?

Certainly, there can be a bad side to faith: a person who has given up on reason and who 'just believes' is easily controlled by his or her religious masters. Such people can easily be persuaded to do bad things, including killing those who don't agree with them.

GO KILL THE UNBELIEVERS!

The 'faith' of such a religious fanatic is clearly not a very good thing.

A good side to faith

But there's no doubt that religious faith can also be a force for good. Faith in God has helped some people deal with the terrible things they have experienced.

And it has inspired many generous and noble acts (though of course it's not just those with faith who behave generously and nobly). Across the globe, people of faith are busy helping others.

Indeed, religious faith has utterly changed some people's lives for the better.

BEFORE   AFTER

Is it reasonable to believe in God?

But while religious faith can be a force for good, the question remains whether belief in God is reasonable.

Tom looks out over the black waters.

Tom: So you really don't believe in God?

Aisha: I'm afraid not. I can no more make myself believe in God than I can make myself believe in Santa Claus. There's no reason to suppose the universe had a creator. And, even if it did, it's perfectly clear its creator isn't the being you call God.

Tom: I disagree. God exists! It is a reasonable thing to believe. Give me a little while, and I'll think of a better argument...

Can you think of a better argument?

Chapter 5

Is time travel possible?

Brad Baddely's rescue

The clouds part and the time machine splutters to a halt, gyrating wildly in the air. Captain Brad Baddely of the time commandos struggles manfully with the joystick as it bucks violently in his hands.

MUST... GAIN... CONTROL... NNGH!

Finally, he gains control and settles his dying machine clumsily on the muddy ground.

Baddely peers through the cockpit window. It's difficult to make out the terrain through the rivulets of rain. He opens the hatch and steps out into a bleak and storm-ravaged landscape.

'So this is planet Vargy,' he whispers to himself. Baddely knows he will soon be dead. There is no way he can repair the failed doobriemat on his time machine. And in just a few minutes' time Planet Vargy will be hit by a huge comet, annihilating everything on its surface.

The time commando scans the horizon. No signs of life. Baddely lets his mind drift wistfully back to Earth, to the family he will never see again.

Suddenly there's a noise: the shriek of another time machine zooming in overhead. The gleaming teardrop glides down and lands gently in the mud beside him.

The hatch springs open.

'Hey! Get in!' The voice from inside sounds oddly familiar. A head peers round the door. Baddely is astonished to find himself looking into a face exactly like his own.

'Who are you?' asks Baddely.

'I've come to rescue you! Quick, hop in and let's get out of here!'

Within a few seconds both time commandos are safely aboard, the time machine sweeping gracefully into the air before accelerating into outer space.

Baddely stares at Planet Vargy in the rear monitor. The comet strikes the surface of the planet, creating a wall of fire that consumes all in its wake.

'Phew! That was a close one. So tell me, who are you?'

'I'm you.'

'Me?'

'Yes. I'm the future you. I've travelled back in time from your future to rescue you. Thank goodness I succeeded!'

'But that's in direct contravention of the time commandos' Prime Directive: No time commando must ever arrange to meet him or herself!'

'Yes. I know. But on this occasion there was no choice. I couldn't let my best buddy – me – get cooked on Planet Vargy, could I? So I travelled back in time to save you. I mean, me.'

Baddely furrows his brow. So he had contravened the Prime Directive, had he? Shouldn't he arrest himself?

Then a faint smile plays across Baddely's lips.

'Well, I won't tell if you won't.'

'It's a deal. But just remember that in a week's time you must travel back to Planet Vargy as it was ten minutes ago to save yourself.'

'What if I forget?'

'You won't. After all, I'm here, aren't I?'

Baddely dropped himself off at the nearest time commando space station.

'Good luck in saving yourself!' shouts Baddely's rescuer as he pilots the time machine back into the air.

'Good luck?' mutters the rescued Baddely to himself. 'Don't need it! I already know that I'll succeed!'

Baddely watches the time machine manoeuvre through the airlock before it streaks back to the future.

'Goodbye, amigo!'

Is time travel illogical?

Kobir and Carol are watching Kobir's favourite show – *The Time Commandos* – on TV.

Kobir: Wow! Great episode!

Carol: It's drivel! It doesn't even make sense.

Kobir: It made sense to me.

Carol: Time travel is illogical. It involves all sorts of logical *contradictions*.

Carol believes that the very idea of time travel is simply confused. She thinks it's *illogical*, which is just to say that it involves *logical contradictions*.

What's a logical contradiction? It's a claim that contradicts itself. Here's an example. If I say: "I am two metres tall and I am not two metres tall," then I have contradicted myself. I am claiming that something is true – that I am two metres tall – but I'm also claiming that it's not true. And it's impossible for a claim to be both true and not true.

Here's another example. Suppose someone claims that there might be round squares somewhere in the world. They go off to look for them.

WE'RE ON AN EXPEDITION TO SEE IF THERE ARE ANY ROUND SQUARES IN ANTARCTICA.

ICE-BOUND

Of course, we *know in advance* that they won't find any, don't we? But why?

Because the very idea of a round square is illogical. A circle, by definition, does *not* have straight sides. A square, by definition, does. So a round square would have to both have straight sides and not have straight sides. And that's a contradiction.

Notice that when a claim is illogical, we don't have to go and observe the world to check whether or not it's true. We can know *just by thinking about* it that it's not true.

Now Carol, like a number of philosophers, thinks the same is true of time travel. She thinks that the *very idea* of people travelling through time – as they do on *The Time Commandos* – involves contradictions. So we can know *just by thinking about it* that time travel is impossible.

But there are other philosophers who, like Kobir, believe that time travel is perfectly logical. Perhaps the universe won't allow time travel. That's something that *science* will have to investigate. But, according to these philosophers, there's certainly no *contradiction* involved in supposing that people might travel through time.

So who is correct, Kobir or Carol? In this chapter we're going to get to grips with some important arguments – arguments that some of the world's leading philosophers and scientists are grappling with right now.

Baddely has and has not been rescued

Let's begin by finding out why Carol thinks time travel is illogical. She starts to explain.

Carol: Look, Baddely is supposed to travel back in time to save himself. But that means at the moment when both Baddelys are standing there on planet Vargy, it's both true that Baddely has already been rescued and not true that he has already been rescued. Right?

Kobir: Hmm. I guess it is.

Carol: After all, it's true that if we asked the just-crashed Baddely whether he has already been rescued from planet Vargy yet, he will say no. The rescue has yet to take place. But if we ask the other Baddely whether he has been rescued yet, he will say yes, he remembers it well. After all, if the rescue hadn't already happened to him, then he wouldn't have been able to travel back to the present.

Carol is correct: it does seem as if it's both true and not true that the rescue has already happened.

Kobir: That's correct, I guess.

Carol: Well, then, *there is a contradiction, isn't there?*

Kobir: It does *seem* like a contradiction, yes.

Carol does appear to have discovered a contradiction in the story about Baddely. And if there's a contradiction, then the story is illogical. It's no more possible for this episode of *The Time Commandos* to be true than it is for a round square to exist.

But *is* there a contradiction?

Two sorts of time

But Kobir is not convinced there's really a problem.

Kobir: I see what you are getting at. But actually, now I think about it, I don't think there is a contradiction.

Carol: Why not?

Kobir: We just need to distinguish between *two sorts of time*.

Carol: Two sorts of time?

Kobir: Yes. Some philosophers distinguish between *personal time* and *external time*.

Carol: What's personal time?

Kobir: Personal time is what gets measured by, say, *Baddely's own wristwatch*. For the Baddely that does the rescuing, his rescue took place in the past in his personal time. It's part of his personal history.

Carol: So what's *external* time?

Kobir: External time is the time that gets measured by, say, a *clock ticking away in orbit around Planet Vargy*. Baddely uses his time machine to travel backwards in external time, the time measured by that ticking clock. But even as he travels backwards in external time he is still travelling forward in his personal time.

Carol: I see. So why is there no contradiction?

Kobir: Well, you said that, as the two Baddelys stand there on the surface of Planet Vargy, it's both true and not true that the rescue has already happened. Right?

Carol: Yes. For one the rescue has happened. For the other it has yet to happen. And that's a contradiction.

Kobir: But that's *not* a contradiction. For as the two Baddelys stand there at the *same point* in *external* time, they are at *different points* within their *personal* time. Their wristwatches tell quite different times, don't they?

Carol: Of course.

Kobir: So what lies in one Baddeley's future lies in the other's past.

Carol: Correct.

Kobir: But there's nothing contradictory about *that,* is there? It can be true that something *hasn't* happened at one point in a person's history, and also true that it *has* happened at another, later point in his or her history. That occurs all the time, doesn't it? What's in a person's future ends up in his or her past. Right?

IT'S THE 21ST OF JANUARY.

NO, IT'S ONLY THE 15TH.

Carol: I guess so.

Kobir: So you see, there's no contradiction!

What is it like to travel in time?

Carol sees that perhaps Kobir has explained away the appearance of a contradiction. But she thinks she's spotted another problem with *The Time Commandos.* She's not sure if they *really* travel in time at all.

Carol: OK, maybe you're right. Maybe there's no contradiction involved in supposing that, as the two Baddelys stand there on the surface of Planet Vargy, it's true that the rescue has taken place, and also true that it hasn't.

Kobir: I *am* right!

Carol: But there's *another* problem with the claim that Baddely travels in time.

Kobir: What problem?

Carol: OK, think about this question: what happens when Baddely travels forward in time? How does it *seem* to him?

Kobir: You mean, what does he see going on around him?

Carol: Yes.

Kobir: Well, in episode one of *The Time Commandos*, when Baddely first uses the time machine, it's parked in a huge hangar. The gleaming time machine is in the centre, surrounded by technicians and lots of complicated-looking machinery. Baddely climbs aboard and shuts the hatch. He sits in the pilot's chair. Then he pushes the time joystick forward very slightly to see what will happen.

Carol: And what *does* happen?

Kobir: The machine stays where it is. But it starts to accelerate forward in time.

Carol: So what does Baddely *see*?

Kobir: When Baddely looks out of the window he sees the technicians buzzing around like flies. The sun starts to shoot rapidly across the sky. Clouds scud past the open hangar door like birds. Everything *speeds up*. Like when you fast-forward a video.

Carol: And when he pushes the stick *further* forward?

Kobir: When he pushes the stick forward some more, things go faster still. Night and day flash past in seconds. The technicians move so fast they become a blur, and then invisible. It's only when Baddely pulls the joystick back to the centre position that things return to normal speed.

Baddely gets really, really slow

Carol now asks Kobir what it's like for the technicians watching Baddely's time machine.

Carol: Fantastic! But now what do the technicians watching the time machine see when Baddely first pushes the joystick forward?

Kobir: I guess Baddely and his machine disappear with a 'Pop!' as he sets off on his journey into the future.

Carol: But *that* can't be right, can it? If Baddely can see what's going on outside his machine as he travels forward in time, then that is because he is *still in the hangar*. Right?

Kobir: I guess so.

Carol: But if he is *still in the hangar*, then he *doesn't* disappear with a 'Pop!' does he? If he can still see the technicians around him, then he's still there to be seen by them.

Kobir: Weird. I guess that's true.

Carol: Only, from their point of view, Baddely will seem to be moving *very, very slowly!*

Kobir: Bizarre!

Surely Carol is right. If Baddely is there to see the other technicians, then they must also be able to see him. And if they are moving very quickly relative to Baddely, then Baddely is moving very slowly relative to them.

Carol thinks this shows that Baddely doesn't *really* travel in time at all. She explains by telling Kobir about another strange device…

Stepping into the slow box

Carol: It's as if Baddely has stepped into the *slow box.*

Kobir: The slow box?

Carol: Yes. I saw a science fiction film the other night called *The Slow World of Doctor Calculus.* In the story, a scientist – Doctor Calculus – discovers how to make a device which, when you step inside it, slows down all the physical processes going on in your body. Step into the box and you grind almost to a halt. Your heart beats only once a minute. The electrical activity in your brain slows to a snail's pace.

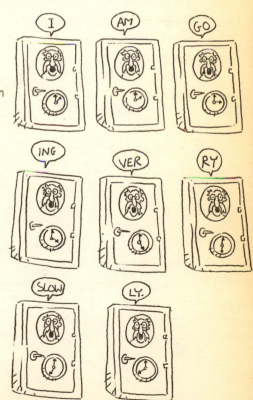

To everyone around you, you seem like a statue. Try to talk to them and they will hear only a very low-pitched hum coming from your

open mouth.

Kobir: How did it seem to Doctor Calculus when he stepped into the box?

Carol: Well, from *his* point of view, everything seemed to *speed up*. People would buzz about like flies. Their voices became high-pitched squeaks. The sun would shoot across the sky.

The world was a blur of frantic activity for as long as Doctor Calculus

stayed in the box.

Kobir: Strange. But what has the slow box got to do with Baddely's adventure?

Carol proceeds to explain.

Carol: It seems to me that Baddely's time machine is really *just another slow box*. It's just as if he has stepped inside Calculus's device.

Kobir: Why?

Carol: Because Baddely never leaves the hangar. He stays right there. He just starts to function *very, very slowly* compared to those around him. From the technicians' point of view, when Baddely touches the joystick, he freezes like a statue. All that's happened is that he's now moving very, very slowly. And when Baddely slowly pushes the joystick forward some more, he starts moving even more slowly. Eventually, after several weeks of hanging around waiting, the technicians watch as Baddely finally gets the joystick back to its centre position and starts to move at normal speed again.

Kobir: I guess that's right.

Carol: But if all that's happened is that Baddely has been slowed down a lot, then *he hasn't really travelled through time at all, has he?*

Kobir: Hmm. Perhaps not.

Carol appears to be right. Certainly, Baddely and the other time commandos aren't supposed just to *slow down* when they go off on their time-travelling adventures. Yet it seems that this is all Baddely's time machine *really* succeeds in doing. It turns out it's just another slow box.

Carol: So you see, *The Time Commandos* is a very confused television programme! It pretends that people are travelling in time when actually they aren't!

Time hopping

Kobir scratches his chin. He's inclined to agree that there's more to time travel than just slowing down.

Kobir: You may be right about the slow box. It isn't *really* a form of time travel, is it? Certainly, a slow box won't allow you to travel *backwards* in time, as Baddely's time machine is supposed to.

Carol: True.

Kobir: But, even if there *is* a problem with the story in *The Time Commandos*, perhaps time travel is still possible. Perhaps what would *really* happen if you started to travel forwards in time is that you would *instantly* find yourself at a different point in time. Dial in 2:45 pm on 1 March 2090 and press the 'travel' button and 'Pop!' there you are, immediately transported to that moment in the future. I don't see that there's anything confused about the suggestion that someone might 'travel in time' in *this* sense.

Carol: Maybe not.

Kobir: In the slow box, Calculus continues to exist at all the points in time in between when he steps in and when he steps out. People outside the box can *still see him in there*. But I guess the machines in *The Time Commandos* don't work like that. They move from one point in time to another *without having to exist at all the moments in time in between*. They simply disappear with a 'Pop!' and reappear with another 'Pop!' in the distant future or past. It's as if they *hop* or *leap* from one point in time to another. You could call it 'time hopping'.

Kobir's suggestion that time machines might work by 'time hopping' does avoid the problem that Carol has been discussing: that Baddely's machine seems otherwise not to be a time machine, but merely a slow box.

Kobir: I admit that the episode where Brad Baddely saw the people around him buzzing about like flies as he travelled forwards in time was a bit confused. But it was only confused in supposing that that's how time travel would *look* from Baddely's point of view. It *wasn't* confused in supposing that time travel makes sense.

Changing the past: the strange case of Queen Victoria's pogo stick

Carol is flummoxed. She remains convinced that time travel *is* illogical. But so far she has struggled to show why. She now has another idea.

Carol: We have overlooked the most famous problem with time travel. A time machine would allow people to *change the past*. And that *really* is illogical.

Kobir: Why?

Carol comes up with an example.

Carol: It's false that Queen Victoria rode a pogo stick during her long reign. Correct?

Kobir: Of course it is. Pogo sticks hadn't even been invented back in Victoria's day.

Carol: But if we had a time machine, we could take a pogo stick back to 1840 and present it to Queen Victoria. She could ride the pogo stick. And so the course of history would be changed.

When we travel back to the present day, we would find that it is now *true* that Queen Victoria rode a pogo stick. We might even discover pictures of her riding the stick.

Kobir: True.

Carol: The past would have *changed*. But it makes no sense to suppose that the past might be altered in that way.

Kobir: Why?

Carol: Well, there's a contradiction, isn't there? It's false that Queen Victoria rode a pogo stick. But also true. That's a contradiction.

Kobir: It *was* false that she rode one. But we have *changed* the past, so it's now true. I still don't see why that's illogical.

Carol: You don't?

Kobir: No. In fact in *The Time Commandos,* Captain Baddely goes back and changes the past *all the time*. In episode one millions of people are wiped out by a virus that a terrorist put in the water supply. Baddely and the other time commandos travel back in time and prevent the terrorist attack from happening.

Come to think of it, changing the past is *exactly* the reason the time commandos were created in the first place. The future Earth Government wanted a unit trained to travel back in time and prevent that terrorist disaster from occuring.

Shooting grandad

As Kobir still can't see what's illogical about changing the past, Carol comes up with another example.

Carol: OK, if Baddely can *change* the past, then he could go back in time and *prevent himself from existing*, couldn't he?

Kobir: You mean, by, say, going back in time and shooting his grandparents prior to the birth of his parents?

Carol: Exactly. If Baddely can change the past, then he could travel back to a time before his grandfather even met his grandmother, hide in the bushes outside his grandfather's house, and then shoot him dead.

Now if Baddely succeeds in preventing his
grandparents from ever meeting, then one
of his parents will never be born. And if
one of his parents won't be born, then
Baddely cannot be born either. So by
travelling back in time *it would be
possible for Baddely to prevent
his own birth.*

BADDELY SHOOTING HIS GRANDAD.

Kobir: And that's illogical?

Carol: Certainly. In order to go back
and prevent his birth, Baddely would
need to have been born. But if he
succeeds in preventing his birth, then
he won't be born.

Kobir: I see the problem. If Baddely is born then he
isn't. But if he isn't then he is. Either way, there's a contradiction.
Either way, he's both born and not born.

Carol: Precisely. So you see, *time travel is illogical.* It generates
contradictions!

Preventing the terrorist attack

Kobir can see what Carol is getting at.

Kobir: Actually, now you mention it, I think there may be a similar
problem with episode one of *The Time Commandos*: the episode
where Baddely and the other time commandos travel back in time to
prevent that terrorist attack. Baddely travels back and succeeds in
stopping the terrorist. The only problem is, as the time commandos
were only created because the terrorist attack happened, by
preventing the attack, Baddely must prevent the time commandos
from being created! But if they aren't created, then the attack *will*
go ahead.

Carol: You're right. That's illogical. If the terrorist attack happens, then it doesn't happen. But if it doesn't happen, then it does. Either way, it happens and it doesn't happen. So, either way, there's a contradiction!

Parallel futures

Has Carol really shown that time travel is illogical? Some philosophers and scientists have suggested that this sort of contradiction can be avoided if we suppose that there are *parallel futures*. Here's how the parallel universe suggestion works.

When Baddely goes back in time and prevents the terrorist attack, he actually creates a *new* future in *addition* to the one from which he travelled. So there is no longer a single future in which the terrorist attack both does happen and doesn't happen. That would be a contradiction.

Rather, there are now *two* futures. In one future, the terrorist attack happens, leading to the time commandos going back in time. But when they prevent the attack, they create a second, parallel future in which the attack never happens. It's this future to which Baddely and the other commandos return.

Now because the two futures are separate, there's no contradiction. There's no future in which the attack both happens and doesn't happen.

Compare this case: it *can* be true both that it's raining and that it isn't raining if we are talking about *two different places*, can't it? The contradiction disappears once we explain that we mean it's raining in one place but not in another.

Similarly it *can* be true both that the terrorist attack happens and that it doesn't happen if we are talking about *two different futures*.

A problem with parallel futures

While some philosophers and scientists think that parallel futures are possible, it turns out these parallel futures would rather undermine the whole point of the future Earth Government creating the time commando team.

Think about it: the future Earth Government creates the time commandos to prevent a terrorist attack that has killed millions of people. The commandos travel back in time and prevent the attack. But they only prevent it from happening *in a parallel future*. In the future from which the time commandos come – the future in which the Earth Government creates them – *the attack still happens.*

So from the point of view of the Earth Government that sent them, the mission is a failure. Millions still die!

Time travel without changing the past

The time commando stories do seem confused. But even if it isn't possible to *change* the past, maybe it's still possible to travel back in time and *make things happen*.

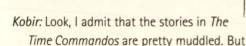

Kobir: Look, I admit that the stories in *The Time Commandos* are pretty muddled. But I'm not sure that you have really shown that time travel is illogical.

Carol: Why not?

Kobir: Well, perhaps we can't go back and *change* the past. Maybe the past is set in stone and cannot be altered. But still, we might go back and have an effect on how the past was originally set. We could go back and make something happen that *did in fact happen*.

Carol: For example?

Kobir thinks for a moment.

Kobir: OK, take the death of Elvis. We think that Elvis died in 1977, don't we? Now suppose that we get in a time machine and travel back to 1973.

Then we shoot Elvis dead.

Carol: But then we *would* have changed the past. Elvis died on 16 August 1977.

Kobir: But *did* he? Maybe people just *think* he did. But perhaps he was actually shot dead in 1973, and his record company, not wanting to lose millions, employed a lookalike – an imposter – to take his place for those last few years.

Carol: Oh. I see. So we don't *change* the past. We simply make something happen *that did in fact happen.*

Kobir: Yes! It's *already* true that Elvis died in 1973. We're not changing anything. There's no problem about doing *that*, is there?

Carol: I guess not.

Trying very hard to shoot Grandad

Carol sees that there's no contradiction involved in Kobir's Elvis time travel story. But she still thinks that time machines must be impossible. She thinks that whether or not we do use them to change the past, and so create contradictions, we *could* do. That rules them out on logical grounds.

Carol: OK, I admit there's no contradiction involved in your story about shooting Elvis. Your story doesn't involve us *changing* the past. But the fact is, time machines *would* also allow us to *change* the past, and in a way that *would* create logical contradictions.

Kobir: Would they?

Carol: Yes, they would. For example, whether or not you *do* decide to go back and kill your granddad, you *could* go back and kill him, couldn't you? And that *would* create a contradiction, wouldn't it?

But Kobir doesn't see why such time machines would *have* to allow us to create contradictions.

Kobir: I don't see why time machines *must* give us the ability to generate contradictions. Suppose I do try to use a time machine to go back in time and shoot Grandad prior to his meeting Grandma. Suppose I actually try my *very hardest* to generate a contradiction!

What we know is that, *no matter how hard I try, I must fail*! Instead of transporting me, the time machine may blow up.

Or my gun may jam at the last minute.

Or I may succeed only in injuring my grandad.

Or I may accidentally shoot the wrong person.

We know that, *somehow* or other, I won't manage to kill Grandad.

Is Carol right? Does the impossibility of our *changing* the past show that time travel is impossible? Or has Kobir shown that time travel might still be possible after all?

I have to admit, I'm just not sure.

Time machines

Carol and Kobir have taken a long, hard look at time travel. So far, I don't think Carol has managed to come up with a good argument to support her claim that time travel is illogical.

True, certain *stories* about time travel don't make much sense. But I'm not at all sure that time travel *itself* is illogical.

Might we one day build machines that allow us to travel into the future or the past? Might you go back and watch dinosaurs feeding?

Might you travel forward billions of years and watch the destruction of the Earth from space?

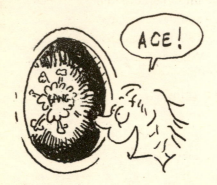

Many science fiction stories are based on the assumption that such machines might eventually be built.

But is time travel *really* possible? Does the idea even make sense?

What do you think?

Chapter 6

Could a machine think?

Thinking

This is me.

And this is a table lamp.

One important difference between me and the table lamp is, of course, that I can think.

What do I mean by 'think'?

Well, for a start, I can do simple sums.

And I can figure out the answers to puzzles.

I can also *understand* language. When I hear other people speaking, I don't just hear noises coming out of their mouths.

I can grasp the meaning of what they are saying.

And of course, understanding language as I do, I can answer them right back.

Unlike a table lamp, I also *enjoy experiences*. I'm eating an apple while I type this. I can taste its rather bitter flesh, smell its slightly sweet aroma, and feel its waxy surface pressed against my finger tips.

I also feel emotions. Sometimes I'm happy and exhilarated. Other times I feel angry.

These are the sorts of things I am talking about when I say I can *think*. I have a rich inner mental life full of all sorts of thoughts and feelings.

A table lamp, on the other hand, can't think. In fact it hasn't got a mind at all. Could a machine think?

We know that flesh and blood humans like ourselves can think. And we know table lamps can't. A table lamp is just a simple piece of machinery. By a *machine*, I mean a man-made device. Toasters, irons, cars and watches are all machines.

But what about *other* sorts of machine? Might they be able to think?

Do pocket calculators think?

Take pocket calculators, for example. They can do *one* of the things I can do with my mind. They can perform mathematical calculations. So do they think?

Actually, it doesn't sound right to me to say that a pocket calculator *thinks*. Surely a bit more is required for thinking. Surely, in order to think, you need a *mind*. And it seems to me that in order to have a mind you need to be able to do a bit more than just do sums. There's far too much that pocket calculators *can't* do. For example, they can't enjoy experiences or have hopes and desires. All they can do is add up the figures that we punch into them. That's not enough for a mind.

Could a supercomputer think?

So I don't believe that pocket calculators can think. But what about other, more complex machines? What about powerful super-computers? Can they think?

Many people would say: no. A supercomputer is really just a very sophisticated calculator: a sort of big pocket calculator.

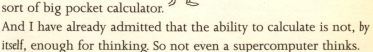

And I have already admitted that the ability to calculate is not, *by itself*, enough for thinking. So not even a supercomputer thinks.

But is that true?

Could a robot think?

Even if supercomputers can't think, perhaps other machines
might. What about *robots*, for example?

Suppose that one day
robots are built that can
walk and talk much as we
do. They are built to
behave just like
humans. They seem to
understand what we say
to them. They even seem
to have emotions, hopes,
desires and so on. They talk
about what they want to do.

They appear
to be happy.

Sometimes they even seem angry.

Would *these* machines think? Would *they* have minds?

That's the question we are going to look at in this chapter.

Tim's new robo-friend arrives

Meet Tim.

It's the year 2500, and Tim has just received a large box through the post. His friend Ed wonders what it could be.

Tim: Ah. It's here at last!
Ed: What is it? It looks huge.
Tim: It's my new friend, Robo-Freddie.
Ed: Robo-Freddie?

Tim tears off the brown paper to reveal what appears to be a young man sleeping inside a large cellophane-fronted box. On the front of the box it says 'Robo-Freddie – your mechanical pal! Indistinguishable from the real thing'.

Tim: He's my new robot buddy. Wow! He
    looks so real. I can't wait to wake him up.

Ed is shocked.

Ed: You've ordered a *robot friend*?
Tim: Yes. Remember you said you couldn't
    come snowboarding with me next
    week? Well, I didn't want to go all by
    myself, so I ordered Robo-Freddie to keep me company. Next week
I'll be whizzing down the snow slopes with Freddie here. He'll be my
new pal.

145

Tim opens the front of the box and picks up Robo-Freddie's remote control.

Tim: All I have to do is press the start button here, and off he'll go!

X-generation sims

Ed walks up to the box and peers closely at the robot inside. Robo-Freddie certainly does look real.

Ed: But this is just a piece of *machinery*. And a piece of machinery can't *really* be your friend, can it? Or, if it can, then why not take the vacuum cleaner instead – it would be much cheaper!

Tim isn't amused.

Tim: Obviously I can't be friends with a vacuum cleaner. After all, a vacuum cleaner can't even talk, can it? But Robo-Freddie can. Robo-Freddie is built to walk, talk and generally behave just like a human being.

Ed: *Just* like a human being?

Tim: Yes. *Just* like a human being. Robo-Freddie is one of the new X-generation sims, the first human simulators that are *absolutely indistinguishable* from the real thing. So I will be able to have conversations with Robo-Freddie, and go snowboarding with him. He even has a mechanical digestive system, so we can go out for lunch together!

Ed: So from the outside it's quite impossible to tell Robo-Freddie from a real human?

Tim: That's right. So you see, while Robo-Freddie may be mechanical, he can still enjoy a day's snowboarding. Just like me.

Robo-Freddie's 'memories'

Ed still isn't convinced that Robo-Freddie will behave exactly like a normal human being.

Ed: Surely Robo-Freddie can't replicate *everything* a human being can do? After all, he has no past, does he? Real human beings have histories that they remember. But Robo-Freddie has no history.

Tim: No, he doesn't.

Ed: Until we turn him on, he won't have experienced anything, so there'll be *nothing for him to remember*. Ask him about his life up to now and he'll have nothing to say. So you see, Robo-Freddie *won't* behave just like a real human.

Tim looks a little smug.

Tim: You're wrong, I'm afraid. Robo-Freddie has no history. But he *does* have memories. Of a sort. X-generation sims like Robo-Freddie come with a choice of pre-programmed memories. Robo-Freddie will think that he's a real human with a real past. He'll remember having a mother and father. He'll remember going to school as a child. He'll remember his fifth birthday, when he got a new red bicycle.

Ed: He will?

Tim points to the manual lying open in Ed's hands.

Tim: Yes. It says so right there in his user's manual. So Robo-Freddie *will* be able to tell us all about his childhood, where he grew up, where he went to school and what he did last week. Just like a real human.

147

Ed: But Robo-Freddie's memories won't be real memories, will they?

Tim: Well, no. His past is a work of fiction. None of it really happened. He never had a fifth birthday. He never got that bike. But Robo-Freddie *won't know that*! So you see? He *will* act just like a normal human being. In fact, there's no way you can tell he isn't human.

Ed: So no one will be able to tell he's a robot? Not even *him*?

Tim: Exactly. If you were to tell Robo-Freddie that he's a robot, he'd laugh at you and tell you not to be so silly.

Does Robo-Freddie have a mind?

Ed feels slightly upset that Tim is replacing him with a machine. But he also feels that, by going on holiday with a piece of plastic-and-alloy machinery rather than a flesh and blood human being, Tim is missing out on something vitally important.

Ed: Well, even if Robo-Freddie is outwardly just like a real human, the fact is that he can't be your friend.

Tim: Why not?

Ed: Because he's missing something crucial. On the outside, he is just like a real human being. But he doesn't have a *mind*.

Tim: A mind?

Ed: Yes. When *you* ski down the slopes, you'll be touched by the beauty of the mountains around you. You'll experience the icy blast of air on your cheeks and the crunchy feel of the snow under your board.

You'll feel exhilarated and glad to be alive. When strangers come up to speak to you on the slopes, you will understand what they're saying and be amused by their jokes. You'll have hopes and desires, anxieties and fears.

The problem is, when Robo-Freddie goes snowboarding with you, he won't have *any* of this rich inner life.

Tim: He won't?

Ed: No. He's *outwardly* just like a human being, I admit. But he's an empty shell. He merely *mimics* thought, feeling and understanding. He merely *mimics* someone with hopes and desires, anxieties and fears.

Ed points through the cellophane window at Robo-Freddie's head.

Ed: There's no *mind* in there.

Tim: There isn't?

Ed: No. And, most importantly, he
won't *really* feel any warmth
towards you. His emotions are all
fake. *That's* why he can't *really* be
your friend.

THERE'S NO MIND IN THERE.

Brains vs computers

Is Ed correct? Many would agree that while Robo-Freddie might
seem on the outside as if he has a mind, his 'mind' is really
nothing more than an elaborate, computer-generated illusion.
Yet Tim is convinced Robo-Freddie's mind is as real as his own.

Tim: Look, I admit that Robo-Freddie isn't a real human being. For
human beings are animals, not machines, and Robo-Freddie is most
certainly a machine.

Ed: True.

Tim: But Robo-Freddie *does* have a mind. A *real* mind. Sure, Robo-
Freddie may be made out of a different sort of *physical stuff* from
me. Inside Robo-Freddie's head there are lots of plastic and metal
components. Inside my head there's a brain made out of flesh and
blood. But *so what*? If a flesh and blood brain like mine can produce
this rich inner mental life, then why can't a plastic and alloy
machine? *What does it matter* how we are physically put together
inside?

How computers work

But Ed thinks it *does* matter how Robo-Freddie is put together. In
particular, Ed thinks it matters that inside Robo-Freddie's head
there's a *computer*.

Ed: Look, like any complex machine
  nowadays, Robo-Freddie is run by a
  computer.

Ed jabs a finger towards Robo-Freddie's head.

Ed: There's a computer right there in his head.
  Now let's get clear about how computers work. A computer is, in
  effect, a device for *shuffling symbols*, isn't it?

Tim: What do you mean?

Ed: Well, take the computer that sits in the middle of an automated
  railway system, making the trains run on time. The computer
  receives lots of *input* from the trains and tracks, indicating the
  position, speed and destination of the trains and how the points are
  set. This input takes the form of lots of sequences of *symbols:*
  strings of ones and zeros.

The symbols represent the trains, their position, and so on. The
computer then sends out other sequences of ones and zeros – its
output – that go off down cables to control the trains and points.

These symbols control the trains and points, making all the trains
arrive safely and in good time at their destinations.

Tim: Yes, I know all that.

Ed: Now, the computer running this railway system doesn't *understand* that this is what it's doing, does it? It doesn't understand that a certain sequence of ones and zeros represents a *train*. It doesn't understand that another sequence represents a *set of points*.

Tim: It doesn't?

Ed: No. All the computer does is follow its program, which makes it send out different strings of symbols depending on those it receives. It doesn't know where the symbols it receives come from. And it doesn't know what the symbols it sends out go on to do.

From the computer's point of view, it could be flying a plane or predicting the weather or translating Hebrew into English. It's all the same to the computer, isn't it?

Tim: Hmm. I *guess* so.

Ed looks triumphant.

Ed: Now this is true of *all* computers. Sequences of symbols get fed in. Then, depending on how the computer is programmed, it sends out other sequences of symbols in response. Ultimately, that's all *any* computer does, no matter how sophisticated it is.

Tim: Are you sure?

Ed: Yes. A computer doesn't *understand* anything at all. It just mindlessly, mechanically shuffles symbols according to its program.

Why Ed thinks Robo-Freddie doesn't understand

Tim can see where this is all leading.

Tim: And I guess you're going to say the same about the computer inside Robo-Freddie's head. It also understands nothing.
Ed: Yes. That's *exactly* my point.

Ed points at Robo-Freddie.

Robo-Freddie is, in effect, just another symbol-shuffling computer housed inside a robot body. A computer designed to mimic understanding. But computers really understand *nothing at all*. So Robo-Freddie understands *nothing at all*.

Shank's computer

Is Ed right? Does Robo-Freddie understand nothing? Tim still isn't persuaded that Robo-Freddie lacks understanding, so Ed decides to tell him about a very famous philosophical argument. I call it the *Chinese room argument.*

Ed: I see you're still not convinced. So let me tell you about the Chinese room. It's a famous argument that was devised by the American philosopher John Searle way back in the 1980s.

Back in the 1980s, a computer engineer called Shank developed a computer that could answer simple questions about a story it had been told. For example, if the computer was given a story in which a boy called John climbed a mountain, and it was then asked, 'Who climbed the mountain?', the computer would give the correct reply: 'John'.

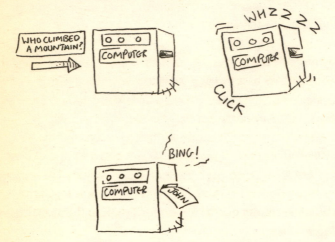

Now some people were very excited by Shank's machine. They claimed it actually *understood* the story it had been told, the questions it received and the answers it gave back.

But Searle disagreed. He thought that, while Shank's computer might *simulate* understanding, it didn't *really* understand anything at all. Searle devised a little story to explain why.

The story of the Chinese room
Ed proceeds to tell Tim all about the Chinese room.

Ed: Suppose a girl, Lucy, is locked in a room. She's given a list of instructions and a sequence of cards with funny squiggly shapes drawn on them. Then Lucy sits by a little hatch through which she's handed more sequences of cards with squiggles on.

Tim: What happens then?

Ed: Lucy's instructions explain how she should shuffle the symbols she has been given. She follows her instructions, and pushes the resulting string of cards back through the hatch.

Tim: I see.

Ed: Now, what Lucy *doesn't* know is that the squiggles drawn on the cards she's given are actually Chinese letters. In fact, the first sequence of cards tells a story in Chinese. The second sequence asks a question about the story. Her instructions allow her to shuffle the two sequences together in such a way that she can give back the right answer to that question.

Tim: Ingenious.

Ed: Now suppose the people *outside* the room feeding in symbols are Chinese. And they don't know what's inside the room. They are likely to think that there must be someone inside the room who understands Chinese, right?

Tim: I guess so. After all, they feed a story and questions, both in Chinese, into the room, and they get correct answers back, also in Chinese. So it must seem to them as if there's someone inside the room who understands Chinese.

Ed: Exactly. Except Lucy *doesn't* understand Chinese, does she?

Tim: No, she doesn't.

Ed: Right. The Chinese room merely *mimics* the behaviour of someone who understands Chinese. Lucy herself is completely unaware that the shapes she is shuffling have any significance. She thinks they're just meaningless squiggles.

Tim: I suppose that's true.

Ed: You see, from Lucy's point of view, whatever *meaning* the symbols have is irrelevant. She's just shuffling them mechanically according to their *shape*.

Tim: And I guess Searle said the same about the computer programmed to answer questions about a story it had been told? Shank's computer didn't *understand* the story or questions. In fact it was unaware that there *was* a story. All it did was to shuffle symbols mechanically according to its program.

Ed: Exactly! It merely *mimicked* understanding. And of course, the same is true of *any* computer.

Ed now points to Robo-Freddie's head.

So the *same is true of Robo-Freddie*. He's just a computer housed in a robot body. A computer programmed to *mimic* the behaviour of a person with a mind. But of course there's no *real* understanding going on in there, as there is in *our* heads. There's just a complex symbol-shuffling device designed to *replicate* understanding.

The right stuff

I have to admit, Searle's Chinese room argument does *seem* very convincing. It does appear to show that no programmed computer could ever understand.

But then *what more* does Searle think is required for *real* understanding? What's the crucial difference between Robo-Freddie and a real human so far as understanding is concerned?

Ed explains.

Ed: In Searle's view, the reason why machines like Shank's computer and Robo-Freddie don't understand is because they're made out of the *wrong sort of stuff*.

Tim: Stuff?

Ed: Yes. Searle doesn't deny that machines can understand. After all, we are a kind of machine, in a way. We are *biological* machines. And we biological machines *can* understand. One day we may even be able to make such biological machines in the laboratory.

HE'S COMING ALONG NICELY.

These man-made machines *would* be able to understand.

Tim: I see.

Ed: The trouble with Robo-Freddie is that he isn't made out of *biological* stuff. Metal and plastic is not the sort of material to use if you want to make a machine that *genuinely* understands. Flesh and blood machines can understand. Metal and plastic machines can't, no matter how complicated they might happen to be.

Is Searle right? Is it true that in order to make a machine that really understands, it needs to be made out of flesh and blood, or perhaps some other sort of biological material, like us?

Robo-Freddie's robo-brain

Tim doesn't believe a word of it.

Tim: Searle is mistaken. His argument *doesn't* show that in order to have a mind, you have to be made out of a certain sort of material.

Ed: Why not?

Tim: Look, suppose I agree, for the sake of argument, that no programmed symbol-shuffling computer can understand. That doesn't mean that Robo-Freddie here can't understand.

Ed: Why not?

Tim: Well, for a start *Robo-Freddie doesn't contain a symbol-shuffling computer.*

This comes as a bit of a surprise to Ed.

Ed: He doesn't?

Tim: No. Take a closer look at the user manual you hold in your hands. Robo-Freddie is one of the new generation human-simulators. According to his user's manual, Robo-Freddie is run, not by a programmed computer, but by one of the new *Robo-Brains*.

Ed: Robo-brains? What are they?

Tim: Well, you know that a
human brain is made out
of millions of cells called
neurons?

Ed: Of course.

Tim: These neurons are woven
together to form an
incredibly complex web.
And this web is buzzing
with electrical activity.

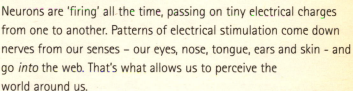

Neurons are 'firing' all the time, passing on tiny electrical charges
from one to another. Patterns of electrical stimulation come down
nerves from our senses – our eyes, nose, tongue, ears and skin - and
go *into* the web. That's what allows us to perceive the
world around us.

Other patterns of electrical
impulse are *sent out* by the web
to control our arms, legs and so
on, making us walk and talk.

Ed: Yes, yes. I already know all about that.

Tim is right. A brain is an incredibly complex
network of neurons all spliced together. This network receives
electrical stimulation from our senses. And it transmits electrical
stimulation out to control our bodies.

Tim points to Robo-Freddie's user manual.

Tim: Now it says in that manual that *Robo-Freddie's robo-brain works in
the same way.* Where we have neurons woven together to form a
web, Robo-Freddie has robo-neurons woven together to form a web.

Ed: Robo-neurons?

Tim: Yes. Robo-neurons are tiny electrical devices that behave in the exact same way as real neurons.

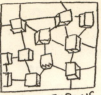

REAL NEURONS   ROBO-NEURONS

A robo-neuron does the exact same job a real neuron does. It sends out the exact same patterns of electrical stimulation.

Ed: So a robo-brain made out of robo-neurons will behave just like a real brain?

Tim: That's right. The exact same sort of electrical activity takes place inside it.

Ed rubs his chin gently. He looks a little bemused.

Ed: I see. So there's no *symbol-shuffling computer* in Freddie's head?

Tim: No. Forget about symbol-shuffling. We are talking about a machine that is structured *exactly like a human brain*. It's just made out of different sort of stuff.

Ed: I see.

Tim: That's why Searle's Chinese room argument isn't relevant here. Even if Searle's argument *does* show that no symbol-shuffling computer can understand, it doesn't show that Robo-Freddie here can't understand. For *Robo-Freddie doesn't contain a symbol-shuffling computer*. His artificial brain works in quite a different way. It works the same way a *real* brain does.

It seems Tim is correct. If Robo-Freddie has a robo-brain, then there's no symbol-shuffling going on in his head. No more than there is in an ordinary flesh and blood brain.

Meat vs metal and plastic

But Ed won't give up. He still thinks that Robo-Freddie can at best only *simulate* feeling, thought and understanding.

Ed: I'm sorry, but the fact is that Robo-Freddie here is an empty shell. He merely outwardly *replicates* a being with a mind.

Tim: I know that's what you *believe*. But what's your *justification* for claiming that Robo-Freddie has no mind? What's your *argument* for supposing he has no thoughts or feelings?

Ed remains convinced that Robo-Freddie is just an empty shell.

Ed: I just can't for the life of me see how you could produce what I have – a mind filled with understanding, thoughts, feelings and emotions – simply by gluing some bits of plastic and metal together.

Actually, Ed is right: it really is difficult to grasp how, simply by putting some bits of plastic and metal together in a particular way, you could create thoughts and experiences. How, just by fitting some mechanical components together, could you possibly create a mind? How do you make an *emotion* out of silicon chips? How do you build a *feeling* out of metal and plastic?

But while it may be difficult to understand how a lump of metal and plastic might have a mind, it is, of course, no less difficult to understand how a lump of meat might have a mind. For, after all, that's just what a brain is: a lump of meat.

Tim: Hmm. I agree. It *is* difficult to understand how that's possible. But then it's no less difficult to see how you could build a conscious mind by weaving *strands of meat* together, is it? As we know that a lump of flesh and blood *can* have a mind, why suppose that lumps of plastic and metal are any different?

Tim's point is a good one. Really, Ed's worry is about how *any* physical thing might come to have a mind, be it a plastic and metal thing or a flesh and blood thing. But then Ed's worry can hardly be used to justify the conclusion that while flesh and blood machines can have minds, metal and plastic machines can't.

Tim's neuron–swap argument

Ed has yet to come up with a good argument to support his claim that Robo-Freddie has no mind. And in fact, as Tim now explains, there's a pretty good argument to support Tim's belief that Robo-Freddie *does* have a mind. I call it the *neuron-swap argument*.

Here's how it goes.

Tim: Look, you think you are inwardly aware of *something* – thoughts, feelings, understanding and so on – something that Robo-Freddie, with his plastic and metal neurons, lacks. Correct?
Ed: Yes. He merely *simulates* thought, feeling and understanding.
Tim: But now suppose that, over the course of a year, surgeons were gradually to replace your organic neurons with robo-neurons like

Robo-Freddie's. Suppose that each week, about two per cent of your neurons are replaced, so that, after one year, you have a robo-brain just like Robo-Freddie's. What do you think would happen to your mind?

Ed thinks for a moment.

Ed: Well, as more and more of my fleshy neurons were replaced with plastic and metal ones, I would gradually cease to have a mind. Thought and feeling would slowly melt away. I would eventually end up a mindless shell, just like Robo-Freddie.

Tim: But your thoughts and feelings are something you are inwardly aware of, right? They are something you *know* about.

Ed: Of course they are.

Tim: So if your inner, mental life were to dwindle away like that, you would *notice* it, wouldn't you?

Ed: Of course I would!

Tim: In fact, you would probably say something like, 'Oh no! Over the past few months my mind has gradually been melting away! What's happening to me?!'

Ed: I'm sure I would say that. Yes.

Tim smiles.

Tim: Except you *wouldn't* say anything like that, would you?

Ed: Why not?

Tim: Well, your new robo-neurons do *exactly* the same job as your originals. So, even as your fleshy neurons were replaced by robo-neurons, your brain would continue to operate just as it always has. Right?

Ed: Er, I guess so.

Tim: But as your outward behaviour – including what you say – is controlled by what's going on in your brain, your outward behaviour would remain unaltered too!

Ed: Oh. I see.

Tim: But then you *wouldn't* mention that your mind was melting away, would you?

Ed: Er, I suppose not. No.

Tim: So you see, you *think* you have a mysterious 'something extra' - some sort of inner, mental life – that Robo-Freddie, being a mere machine, lacks. But it turns out that this mysterious 'something extra' doesn't exist! *There's nothing you are inwardly aware of that you would lose if your brain were replaced by a robo-brain!*

This is a very interesting argument. It does seem to show that, while Ed might think that he has something that Robo-Freddie, being made out of plastic and metal, lacks, this mysterious something is an illusion.

Out of the closet

Ed looks confused. He still feels sure that Robo-Freddie's thoughts, feelings and understanding are all a sham. But is he right?

Tim: Look, I see you are *still* not convinced. So I shall tell you something I shouldn't.

Ed: Tell me what?

Tim: Take a deep breath.

Ed is getting irritated.

Ed: What?

Tim: I have something important to tell you.
Ed: What is it?
Tim: Go and take a look in the cupboard over there.

Ed walks over to the cupboard and slowly opens the door.
Inside, he sees a large, cellophane-fronted box.

Tim: Turn on the light.

Ed reaches over and flips the switch in the closet. Suddenly, the
cupboard is flooded with light. Ed staggers back in horror.

Tim: That's right. It's your packaging.

Across the front of the box is written, 'Robo-Eddie – your
mechanical pal! New X-generation sim with robo-brain!'

Ed: It can't be true!
Tim: It is true, Robo-Eddie.
Ed: Don't be ridiculous! I'm a human!
Tim: No. You're a robot. I bought you to take with me on last year's

winter holiday. Only this winter you decided not to come. So I'm replacing you with this year's model.

Ed can't believe what he's hearing.

Ed: I ... I don't understand.
Tim: I think you do. *Still* think that robots can't have minds?

Ed slumps in a chair. His mind is reeling.

Or is it? Does Robo-Eddie have a mind to reel?

What do you think?

Chapter 7

But is it science?

The rise of science

Just a few hundred years ago we had no electricity and no
gas-fired central heating. For my ancestors, day-to-day life was
usually hard, in large part spent just keeping warm, watered
and fed.

People were ignorant, too. They had little knowledge of what
was going on in the world. They thought the Earth was
stationary and that the entire universe was just a few thousand
years old. Plagues and epidemics were thought to have a
supernatural origin. People believed that witches and demons
roamed the land, causing illness and misfortune.

There were no vaccinations, no anaesthetics and very little effective medicine. Without disinfectants, antibiotics or even an understanding of the importance of hygiene, wounds easily turned septic. Infected limbs were sawn off without anaesthetic.

One of the leading forms of medicine involved 'bleeding' people.

Now take a look around your house. Turn a tap and clean fresh water – as much as you want – pours out. Pick up the phone and you can immediately talk to somebody in Australia. A dark room is made bright at the flip of a switch. Your fridge keeps a wide variety of foods from around the world fresh for days on end.

There's a TV, radio and music system to entertain you and tell you about

what's going on across the globe. You will live decades longer than your ancestors, thanks to vaccinations, antibiotics, surgery and the development of new genetic techniques. We regularly fly to different countries and continents in

just a few hours, just for the fun of it. Men have walked on the moon.

Our lives have been utterly transformed. But why?

THE RISE OF SCIENCE!

Because of the rise of science.

Science only really took off about 400 years ago. That's only ten times as long as I have lived! Yet in this short period of time science has changed our lives almost beyond recognition.

Pseudo-science

We have been looking at the short but impressive rise of science. 'All very interesting,' I hear you say, 'but what is science exactly?'

A good question. After all, if science is so wonderful, then it would be very useful if we could say what it actually is. It would also be helpful if we could say what makes for a *good* scientific theory.

But in fact, despite the enormous importance of science to our lives, it's astonishingly difficult to pin down exactly what science is. Even scientists can struggle to explain what distinguishes a good scientific theory from a bad one.

In fact, much that *looks* like science isn't science. Sometimes it's *pseudo-science*.

As you will soon discover, it can be extremely difficult to spot the difference between pseudo-science and the real thing. An *awful* lot of people are regularly duped into believing pseudo-scientific claptrap.

In this chapter we are going to look at one very famous example of pseudo-science. By the end of the chapter, you'll be much better able to spot pseudo-science when you see it.

But before we take a look at pseudo-science, it's worth reminding ourselves of two important facts about science. The first is that there are important limits to science. The second is that the rise of science has involved quite a struggle.

The limits of science

Of course, not *every* scientific discovery has improved our lives. We shouldn't forget that science has also given us pollution and weapons of mass destruction. And let's remember that there are *important questions science can't answer.* For example, science can't answer *moral* questions. It can't tell us how we *ought* to live our lives.

Here's a concrete example. Science will soon allow us to 'design' babies genetically. For example, you might choose to have a baby that is immune to certain diseases, or that is especially intelligent, or has particularly blue eyes. These are things we *will* be able to do. But *should* we? Is it morally OK to design children, much as you might design a new suit or a handbag? Is that a proper attitude to take towards another human being?

> I'D LIKE MY DAUGHTER TO HAVE THOSE EYES, THOSE LIPS AND THAT NOSE.

That is a question science can't help us with.

Still, even if science can't answer all our questions, the fact is it's an enormously powerful tool. It has changed our lives dramatically. That transformation has been almost entirely for the better.

Science and religion

As I say, the rise of science has involved quite a struggle. One of the most famous battles was over the theory that the Earth moves.

Back in the seventeenth century, the Catholic Church was

immensely powerful. It took the
view that we inhabit a stationary
Earth located at the centre of the
universe, with everything –
including the sun – revolving
around us, like this.

Certainly there
are passages in the Bible that
strongly suggest the Earth is
stationary. Psalm 93.1 of the Bible says…

But then the scientists Copernicus and Galileo developed a
scientific theory in which the Earth revolves around the sun.
The Catholic Church condemned Galileo for claiming that his
sun-centred model was true and imprisoned him in his own
home until finally he agreed to withdraw his claim.

But Galileo was right: the Earth *does* move.

Interpreting the Bible

Of course, the vast majority of Christians now accept that Galileo
was correct. So what do they say about passages such as Psalm
93.1?

They say that we should be careful about taking everything
that the Bible says *entirely* at face value. To begin with, let's
remember that while the Bible may be the word of God, it was
written down by humans, and of course humans can and do
make mistakes. Christians may also suggest that many of those
parts of the Bible that *appear* to be contradicted by the findings of
modern science have either been wrongly interpreted, or else
were never meant to be taken literally. After all, the Psalms are
poetry. People don't criticise the poet Wordsworth for writing 'I

wandered lonely as a cloud'
on the grounds that
clouds are incapable of
feeling emotions such as
loneliness.

Poetry isn't meant to be
interpreted entirely
literally. The same might
be said of the Bible.

Creationism

Now let's get back to pseudo-science: stuff that *looks* like science
but isn't. The example I am going to focus on in this chapter
involves *creationism*.

By creationism, I mean the view that the Biblical story of
creation is *literally* true. That, at least, is what most of those who
describe themselves as 'creationists' mean by the term.
Creationists believe that everything described in
Genesis – the first book of the Bible – *really
happened*.

So what does the Bible have to say
about creation? According to Genesis,
God created the universe, including
the Earth and all the different species
of plants and animals, over a period of
six days.

On day one, God created 'heaven and
earth' and night and day.

On day two, He made 'a firmament' which he called 'Heaven' (I'm not really sure what a firmament is). On day three, God created dry land with grass and trees. On the fourth day He created the Sun, Moon, planets and stars and on the fifth day He created fish and fowl.

And on the sixth day, God created cattle and other creatures that crawl on the dry land, including, finally, the first man – Adam – and woman – Eve. God commanded Adam and Eve to be fruitful and multiply and to rule over everything on Earth.

Creationists believe this story is no myth. As I say, they think it really happened. God created the universe and all living species in just six 24-hour days.

But when?

A six-thousand-year-old universe

According to most creationists, God made the universe about *six thousand years ago*. Creationists usually base their calculations of the age of the universe on the generations listed

GOD MADE THE UNIVERSE ON THE MORNING OF THE 3RD OF OCTOBER 4004 B.C.

in the Bible (the passages that say Adam begat Seph who begat Enos and so on). In fact in 1650 James Ussher, an Anglican Bishop, calculated that the universe was created on 3rd October, 4004 years before the birth of Christ.

The increasing popularity of creationism

Creationism is not just of historical interest. It is a living theory. In fact it has seen a vast surge in popularity over the last few decades.

True, in England, where I live, and in the rest of Europe, hardly anyone believes in creationism. But in the United States the situation is very different.

A recent poll conducted in the US indicated that *about 45 per cent of US citizens now believe in creationism.* They really believe that the universe, and all living species, were created in the same week less than ten thousand years ago.

So popular has creationism become that a university teacher from Tennessee recently wrote:

> *Medieval ideas that were killed stone dead by the rise of science three to four hundred years ago are not merely twitching; they are alive and well in our schools, colleges and universities.*

Is creationism scientific?

Why has creationism become so popular?

One of the main reasons is that people have been persuaded that creationism is *good science.*

In fact, in some states in the US, creationism is taught alongside evolution in biology classes. It is presented as an *equally respectable scientific theory.*

Even the current President of the United States, George W. Bush, believes both evolution and creationism should be taught in schools.

If many millions of Americans believe that creationism is scientifically respectable, then perhaps we should look at it a little more carefully. Maybe there is something to the claim that creationism is good science after all?

Let's find out.

The Big Bang/evolution theory

To start with, let's take a quick look at what the overwhelming majority of scientists now believe about how the universe started and how life emerged.

The universe, they say, started between ten and twenty billion years ago with the Big Bang, an unimaginably violent explosion in which matter, space and even time itself came into being.

A billion years is one thousand times a million years, which is itself one thousand times a thousand years. So ten billion years is a very long time indeed. It's hard to get a feel for just *how* long. Try the following little demonstration. Stand about twenty metres from a wall, pointing away from it, like so.

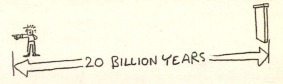

Now imagine that the wall is when the universe began and the tip of your finger is where we are now, with the twenty-billion-year history of the universe stretched out in between.

Then the distance between the tip of your finger and your nose – about a metre – represents *one* billion years. That means that one million years is one millimetre – about the thickness of the skin on the tip of your finger.

So how old is the Earth? Most scientists believe it's approximately four and a half billion years old. That's about four and a half metres back from the tip of your finger.

What of life? Scientists believe the first life-forms emerged on Earth some three and a half billion years ago. That's three and a half metres back from your fingertip.

A process of *evolution* then took place. The simplest life-forms very gradually evolved into slightly more complex life-forms, which in turn evolved into still more sophisticated forms of life. But it took a very long time for anything other than simple microscopic life-forms to appear. In fact the dinosaurs appeared

177

DINOSAURS
APPEAR

only some 230 million years ago: just a little way up your forearm.

And the first large mammals appeared only 65 million years ago: about where your finger joins your hand.

Modern man – *homo sapiens* – appeared perhaps only 200 thousand years ago: that's about one-fifth the thickness of the skin on the tip of your finger.

That gives you some sense of the age of the universe according to the overwhelming majority of scientists.

So where do creationists place the beginning of the universe? They say the universe is less then ten thousand years old. Ten thousand years is just *one hundredth* the depth of the skin on your fingertip.

You can now see that the difference in the age of the universe depending on whether you accept creationism or the Big Bang theory is *absolutely immense*: the difference between the ten to twenty metres stretched out behind you and one hundredth of the depth of skin on the tip of your finger!

As I say, the vast majority of scientists believe the Big Bang/evolution theory. Of course, they disagree about the details. For example, they disagree about *exactly* how evolution took place. And they argue over the *exact* age of the universe.

But that there was a Big Bang many billions of years ago and that life emerged and evolved over millions or billions of years is now accepted by the overwhelming majority of scientists.

Brad and Carol's discussion

Let's now take a closer look at why so many people believe that creationism is good science.

Meet Brad and Carol.

They're sitting in The Magic Café here in Oxford where I live. Brad is a visiting American student. He believes in creationism. Carol is a science student from England (she lives with Aisha – we met her in chapter one).

Carol believes that the universe started with the Big Bang billions of years ago and that life evolved gradually. She thinks creationism is a lot of unscientific claptrap. But Brad believes that creationism is just as good a scientific theory as Carol's Big Bang/evolution theory.

Let's see if we can figure out who is correct, and why.

Evidence against creationism

Carol: You believe the universe is only six thousand years old, that all living things were created at that time?

Brad: That's right.

Carol: Even the dinosaurs?

Brad: Yes.

Carol: So tyrannosaurus rex and the velociraptors roamed the Earth alongside man just six thousand years ago?

Brad: Yes.

Like most creationists, Brad doesn't deny dinosaurs existed. After all, we find their fossils beneath our feet. But of course, if creationism is true, then they too must have been created just six thousand years ago, along with everything else.

Carol: But that's only *one and a half thousand years* before the Ancient Egyptian pyramid of Cheops was built.

Brad: True.

Carol: You're nuts!

Brad: Obviously you don't believe me. But don't be so quick to resort to insults. Tell me *why* you believe creationism is unscientific.

Carol now comes up with three pieces of evidence that she thinks conclusively show that creationism is false. Her first piece of evidence is the *light coming from distant stars.*

Light from distant galaxies

Carol: OK. Take, to begin with, the light and other emissions we observe coming from distant galaxies and other remote objects. These objects are so far away that it would take light millions or billions of years to reach us. So we must see them as they were millions or billions of years ago. See, the universe must be billions of years old!

Brad: I see your confusion. The universe is, in truth, only a few thousand years old. But, when God created the universe, He created the light you're referring to *on its way* to us.

Brad is right: if God created the light quite close to the Earth, so that it would take just six thousand years to get here, then the universe could be just a few thousand years old.

Is God deceiving us?

But Carol thinks she has spotted a problem with Brad's reply.

Carol: But if God created the light *on its way*, then He's deceiving us, isn't He?

Brad: Why?

Carol: Well, God is creating the *illusion* of a very old universe, isn't he? Look, suppose we see a supernova explosion way off in deepest space. It would take the light we see millions of years to get here from that explosion, wouldn't it? Now, according to you, the light we see *didn't* come from any supernova explosion! Actually, it was created *just six thousand years ago*, on its way to us. In fact, because the entire universe is only six thousand years old, then *the explosion we seem to see never really happened*!

Brad: That's all true.

Carol: But then God is deceiving us, isn't He? *He is making it look as if the universe is millions of years old, when it's not!* Its age is an illusion!

Brad: It's merely an illusion, yes.

Carol: But God is supposed to be *good*. Why would He go in for such deliberate deception? Why would He *deliberately* make it seem as if the universe is much older than it is? Why would he deliberately fool us into thinking the supernova explosion happened?

Brad still doesn't see why, by creating the light on its way to us, God would be deceiving us.

Brad: God isn't deliberately deceiving us. It's just that, because the universe and all living things were created fully-formed, that inevitably gives rise to the impression of a longer history. Take, for example, God's creation of Adam: the first man. God created Adam as an adult. But as adults grow up from children, the existence of Adam as a mature adult gives the impression of Adam being older – old enough to have had a childhood. Correct?

Carol: Well, I guess so.

Brad: Or take the existence of the first trees. They were created as mature, fully-grown trees. If Adam cuts down a tree it will turn out to have tree rings, just like any tree. Right?

Carol: I guess so.

Brad: But again, tree rings indicate age, don't they? They show a history of growth. So you see, by creating fully-grown trees, God would have created something that could easily be taken to be older than it really is. The same goes for the light rays that God created on its way to us. God doesn't *deliberately* deceive us. It's just that, because the universe was created fully-formed, it can inevitably give rise to the mistaken impression that it's older than it actually is.

Brad does appear to have dealt with Carol's first piece of evidence against creationism. So Carol tries a different approach.

Craters on the Moon

Carol: OK, here's *another* piece of evidence that the universe is much older than just a few thousand years. Take a look at the Moon and you will see that it's covered in craters.

These craters are caused by meteorite impacts, correct?

Brad: Yes.

Carol: There are countless thousands of craters, aren't there?

Brad: Certainly.

Carol: Yet meteorite impacts on the Moon are rare. The last recorded one was several hundreds of years ago. So the only way the Moon could have acquired that many craters is by being very old indeed.

Brad is ready for this argument.

Brad: Well, again, perhaps the Moon was created with its craters. I have already explained why that wouldn't mean that God is a deceiver.

Carol: Hmm.

Brad: But in any case other explanations are available. Perhaps, six thousand years ago, there was much more debris floating around in space. These space rocks were quickly drawn by gravity to objects like the Moon, causing lots of craters over a short time. Nowadays most of the debris is gone, which is why impacts are currently so rare.

Carol is finding Brad's answers hard to deal with. After all, if there was lots more space debris around six thousand years ago, that really *would* explain all those craters, wouldn't it?

The fossil record

So Carol moves on to her third piece of evidence.

Carol: What about the fossil record? Examination of the rock beneath our feet reveals strata or layers that have been laid down apparently over many millions of years. Fossils of long-dead creatures and plants can be found embedded in these strata. And you find different life-forms fossilized in the different levels. At the lowest levels, only simple creatures are found. Higher up you discover more complex forms, including the dinosaurs. Higher still you find the larger mammals. Only the most recently deposited layers reveal traces of man.

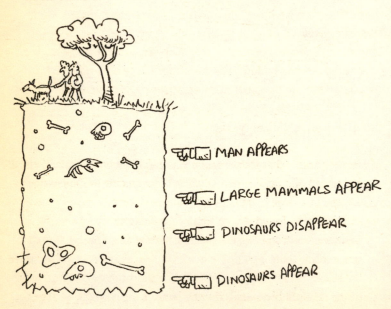

Brad: You're absolutely right: the fossils *are* ordered in that way.

Carol: Now this ordering of the fossil record tallies very well with the theory of evolution, but it seems to contradict the Biblical account on which all life-forms were produced more or less simultaneously less then ten thousand years ago.

Brad: Why do you say that?

Carol: Surely, if creationism was correct, we should expect to find examples of all the different life-forms muddled up throughout the rock layers – assuming, that is, that the few thousand years that have elapsed since creation are enough to allow rock layers even to form. For example, if man and all the other mammals lived alongside the dinosaurs, *there should be fossils of men and women, cows and pigs, elephants and giraffes and other large modern mammals muddled up with dinosaur fossils.*

But the fact is that today, even after millions upon millions of fossils have been dug up, not *one single* well-documented example of, say, a fossil of a large mammal in the dinosaur layers has ever been found. All we find in the dinasaur layer are small, squirrel-like mammals. How do you explain *that*?

Carol looks suitably satisfied with herself.

She thinks she has finally come up with concrete, irrefutable evidence that creationism is false.

Brad's flood theory

Yet Brad remains strangely unperturbed.

Brad: Actually, as a creationist, I *can* explain the fossil record. Quite easily. You see, we creationists believe in the Biblical Flood.

Carol: You mean, the flood on which Noah famously floated his ark?

Brad: Yes. That flood *really* happened. Everything described in the Bible *really happened*. Now, not surprisingly, the rains that caused the Biblical flood caused huge mud deposits.

These mud deposits then solidified and turned into the rock layers we find beneath our feet. What you think of as layers of rock billions of years old are actually just mud deposits a few thousand years old.

Carol: But why do the fossils appear in the order they do?

Brad: Well, the reason one finds the larger, smarter mammals above dinosaurs, for example, is that the mammals are faster-moving and more intelligent than the cumbersome dinosaurs. When the flood came, the larger mammals ran to higher ground and drowned later.

So they got buried later. *That's* why they appear in the higher layers of mud.

This flood explanation of the fossil record is extremely popular among creationists – in fact almost all creationists now believe it. It's even taught in some American schools.

Carol is really beginning to struggle. She's becoming more and more irritated with Brad's replies. Every time Carol puts forward what she thinks is another solid bit of counter-evidence against creationism, it turns out Brad has yet another ingenious explanation up his sleeve. She feels as if she's being tied up in knots.

There are countless more pieces of counter-evidence that Carol *could* wheel out. But she's starting to suspect that Brad will somehow be able to explain them *all* away.

Why Brad thinks creationism is scientific

Brad sees that he is getting the better of the argument. So he sums up his position.

Brad: It seems pretty clear to me that your 'evidence' that the universe is millions or billions of years old is inconclusive.

Carol: Inconclusive?

Brad: Yes. It's becoming clear, isn't it, that my creationist theory is just as 'scientific' as your Big Bang/evolution theory? It's just as good a theory.

Carol: Why do you say that?

Brad: Well, scientists, I take it, use their five senses – the senses of sight, hearing, touch, smell and taste – to observe the world around them. And their job is to construct theories to *fit* and *explain* what they observe around them. Correct?

Carol: Yes.

Brad: Well, we have just seen that my creationist theory *does* fit what has been observed. It fits the evidence just as well as your Big Bang/evolution theory. As I have explained, it *does* tally with the fossil record. It *can* explain the existence of all those craters on the Moon. It *is* consistent with the existence of light from distant stars.

Brad looks triumphant.

Brad: So you see? *My creationist theory is just as scientific as yours!*

Is Brad correct? Is creationism really just as good a theory as the Big Bang/evolution alternative? After all, Brad's theory *does* fit the evidence.

Are dogs spies from the planet Venus?

Actually, Brad's theory isn't at all scientific. But
why not? Why isn't creationism good science?

That's not quite so easy to explain.

Let's take a look at *one* of the problems
with the claim that creationism is good
science.

Suppose I tell you that dogs are spies
from the planet Venus.

That's right, Fido here might look like a harmless
pet, but he's actually a spy gathering information in preparation
for an imminent Venusian attack.

Obviously, you don't believe
me. But why not?

Well, doesn't all the
evidence suggest that
dogs are pretty stupid
creatures incapable of
such treachery? After all,
they can't even talk, can they?
And they have small brains, which
suggest they are pretty dim. Nor do we
find transmitters hidden about our
houses by which our dogs might
transmit their secret reports to
Venus.

So surely, you would no doubt say,
the evidence *overwhelmingly* supports
the theory that dogs are
affectionate and faithful pets, not
spies from another world.

189

Defending the dogs–are–Venusian–spies theory

But hang on a moment. What if, in reply, I claim that while dogs' brains may be small, they're peculiarly efficient. In fact, I suggest, dogs are highly intelligent creatures which *do* possess language. It's just that they cunningly hide their intelligence and linguistic ability from us. And the reason we don't find their radio transmitters secreted about the house is that the transmitters are actually embedded in their brains.

RADIO TRANSMITTER

Now I have made my theory fit the evidence again! I have shown that all your counter-evidence actually fits in with my theory after all!

To this you might reply that an X-ray of a dog's head reveals no radio transmitter. Nor can we detect any transmission coming from their heads. And in any case, we know that Venus is a lifeless planet incapable of producing an invasion force.

PLANET SURFACE

To which I might reply that dog transmitters are made out of organic material that resembles brain tissue, which is why they don't show up on X-rays or in dog autopsies. And dogs transmit via a mysterious medium we cannot yet understand or detect. And as a matter of fact Venus *is* inhabited. It's just that the Venusians live deep below the surface in secret bunkers. That's why we don't know about them.

Notice that, yet again, by adding on a few additional claims, I have made my theory fit the evidence.

You can see how this rather silly game might continue. I can keep on protecting my weird theory about dogs being Venusian spies by constantly adding on new bits to deal with whatever evidence you might come up with.

So the interesting thing about my dogs-are-Venusian-spies theory is that I *can continue to make it fit and explain what has been observed*. I just need to keep on using my ingenuity to add on bits to deal with what might otherwise *seem* to be compelling counter-evidence. But if a good scientific theory is one which fits and explains what has been observed, then surely my theory that dogs are Venusian spies is just as "good" a theory as the common-sense theory that they are merely harmless pets, isn't it?

Reasoning close to madness

Of course not. Pretty clearly, the kind of reasoning that I am using to defend my bizarre theory about dogs is *not* scientific.

In fact you can see that *any* theory, no matter how utterly mad, can be protected in this way for *ever*, no matter how much evidence might be brought against it. If this was a scientifically respectable way of carrying on, then *all* theories would be equally scientifically respectable, including the theories that dogs are Venusian spies, that cheese is made of fairy dust...

...and that Mexicans are the secret rulers of the universe.

Interestingly, the kind of reasoning that I have been using to defend my dogs-are-Venusian-spies theory is symptomatic of certain sorts of mental illness, such as schizophrenia. It's exactly how schizophrenics defend their bizarre beliefs.

It is a form of reasoning that is, quite literally, close to madness. Yet it's exactly this sort of reasoning that Brad has been using to defend creationism. Brad has been playing much the same game that I played in defending my bizarre theory about dogs. Every time Carol comes up with a solid-looking bit of evidence against creationism, Brad just adds a bit more on to his theory to protect it.

What Brad is doing might look a bit like science. After all, it's true that Brad is using his ingenuity to develop a theory that continues to fit the evidence. But Brad's method is unscientific (though of course he's not actually mad).

Confirming theories

Here's another very important difference between creationism and the

THE THEORY OF EVOLUTION IS STRONGLY CONFIRMED..

BECAUSE IT MAKES A CLEAR AND PRECISE PREDICTION...

theory of evolution. The theory of evolution is *strongly confirmed*.

When is a theory strongly confirmed?

Well, to begin with, the theory has got to make *predictions*. It has got to say what we should expect to find when we observe the world around us. And these predictions must be clear and precise.

Second, for a theory to be strongly confirmed, the prediction must be bold. That's to say, the theory must predict something that *we wouldn't otherwise expect*.

A BOLD PREDICTION...

193

Here's an example. The theory of evolution predicts that, when we look under the ground, we will find the fossils of plants and animals arranged in a particular way throughout the rock layers. The lowest layers will have just simple organisms; higher up more complex life-forms will appear, and so on. The layers should show *evolutionary progression*. There should be absolutely no out-of-place fossils, such as a fossil of a man in one of the lowest layers. Not even *one*.

Now, if evolution *wasn't* true – if life on Earth *didn't* evolve – you really wouldn't expect this very precise ordering of fossils. In fact this sort of order would be pretty *unlikely* if evolution didn't take place.

So by predicting this precise order in the fossil record, the theory of evolution predicts *something we wouldn't expect otherwise*. That makes it a *bold* prediction.

A PREDICTION THAT IS TRUE

Finally, in order for a theory to be strongly confirmed, the prediction must be *true*.

Even today, after many millions of fossils have been dug up, not *one single* example of an out-of-place fossil has ever been found. *That very strongly confirms the theory of evolution.*

Is creationism strongly confirmed?

So what about creationism. Is *that* strongly confirmed?

SO WHAT CLEAR, PRECISE AND BOLD PREDICTIONS DOES CREATIONISM MAKE?

ERR....

GENESIS IS TRUE

No, it isn't. For a start, let's ask what clear, precise and bold predictions creationism makes.

The answer appears to be: *none at all*.

Take, for example, the fossil record. What does creationism predict we should find?

194

Creationists are very vague about that. If the fossils were jumbled up in no particular order, they would say: 'See, that fits our theory!' But if the fossils are arranged in exactly the sort of way predicted by the theory of evolution, they say: 'But that fits our theory too!' They claim the flood explains the order of the fossils.

So it doesn't matter *what* we find: the creationists can say it fits their theory. That's because their theory doesn't take any risks with predictions. It makes no bold predictions. In fact it doesn't really predict anything at all.

But then it can never be strongly confirmed.

Why creationism isn't good science

So while creationism might *look* like good science, it isn't. In fact the kind of 'science' practised by creationists is really pseudo-science.

The trouble is, because most of us are very bad at spotting the difference between pseudo-science and the real thing, *lots* of people have been taken in.

True, no scientific theory is ever conclusively proved in the sense that it's proved beyond any possible doubt. There is always the *possibility* of error. But some theories are much better confirmed than others. The fact is that, while scientists might argue over the details, the theory that the universe is billions of years old with life having evolved from very primitive life-forms is *overwhelmingly* confirmed by the available evidence.

Creationism, on the other hand, is overwhelmingly disconfirmed. True, there's always the tiniest *possibility* of error. But it's hardly any more likely that it should turn out that the universe is actually only six thousand years old than it should turn out that the Sun goes round the Earth!

Creationism and Christianity

Of course, to say that creationism is false is not to say that the universe wasn't created by God. Perhaps it was. Even if we reject creationism, we can still be 'creationists' in *that* sense.

Many Christians are. They take the same view about the creation story in Genesis as they do about Psalm 93.1 – the Psalm that says that the Earth doesn't move. They may say that the Genesis story is simply a metaphor or myth. Or they may interpret the Genesis story in a way that makes it consistent with what science has discovered. For example, some Christians suggest that the six 'days' of creation shouldn't be understood as ordinary, 24-hour days, but 'days' lasting many millions of years.

So you can reject creationism while still remaining a Christian. Just as you can deny that the Earth is stationary while still remaining a Christian.

Spotting pseudo-science

We all know that science is pretty wonderful. We are impressed when something is described as 'scientifically proven', 'the latest scientific development' or 'recommended by leading scientists'.

But not everything that pretends to be scientific really is.

In this chapter we have looked at just *one* example of how people can be fooled into thinking that a theory is good science when it's not. But there are many other examples too. I'm sure you can think of some.

Some Useful Words

ARGUMENT In philosophy, an argument consists of one or more claims (often called *premises*) and a conclusion. The premises are supposed rationally to *support* the conclusion.

ASTROLOGY Astrologers claim that the arrangement of the heavenly bodies plays a role in determining what will happen on Earth. Many suppose that we can predict the future by looking at the stars.

ATOM An atom is one of the invisible particles out of which PHYSICAL MATTER is composed.

BIG BANG The huge explosion with which the universe is supposed to have begun.

COMPATIBILISM The view that DETERMINISM is compatible with FREE WILL.

I AM SIX FEET TALL BUT IT'S NOT TRUE THAT I AM SIX FEET TALL.

CONFIRMED A claim is confirmed if there is some EVIDENCE (even if only a tiny bit) that is true.

CONTRADICTION A contradiction is a claim that says that something is true but also is not true.

COUNTER-EVIDENCE EVIDENCE against a claim.

CREATIONISM Usually, those who describe themselves as 'creationists' mean they believe that the account of creation in Genesis is really true: that the world and all species of life were created in just six days by God some time in the last ten thousand years or so. There was no BIG BANG and there has been no EVOLUTION of new species.

DETERMINISM The view that everything that happens in the PHYSICAL UNIVERSE is fixed in advance by the LAWS OF NATURE.

DISCONFIRMED A claim is disconfirmed if there is some EVIDENCE that it is false.

ELECTRON One of the tiny particles out of which ATOMS are made.

ESP Extra-Sensory Perception. Perception other than by the five usual senses of sight, taste, touch, smell and hearing. A sort of 'sixth sense'.

EVIDENCE Evidence is information that rationally supports a belief – makes it more likely to be true. For example, suppose I believe that someone is living in that cottage over there.

The fact that there is smoke coming from the chimney provides evidence that my belief is true.

EVOLUTION Species are supposed to evolve: they

gradually   change   and   adapt

over   many   generations.

FAITH To have faith is to believe even though there may be little if any REASON to believe.

FATALISM The view that what will happen to us is out of our control: it will happen no matter what we might do. So there is no point in our trying to prevent it from happening.

SCRITZH SCRITZH

FREE WILL The ability to *act freely*. For example, I believe that I am now free either to scratch the top of my head or not. There, I scratched my head. But I believe I was able not to scratch my head. I could have done otherwise. To believe in FREE WILL is to believe we can act freely.

GOD The SUPERNATURAL being that, according to Jews, Christians and Muslims, is all-powerful, all-knowing and all-good.

HAEMORRHOIDS Also known as piles. A very painful condition of the bottom.

JUSTIFIED A belief is JUSTIFIED if there is good REASON to suppose that it is true ~ i.e. it is supported by good EVIDENCE and/or ARGUMENT.

LAWS OF NATURE The laws of nature hold throughout the entire PHYSICAL UNIVERSE and determine how PHYSICAL MATTER and energy will behave.

LOGICAL/ILLOGICAL A claim is logical if it involves no logical CONTRADICTIONS. If it does, it is ILLOGICAL. An ARGUMENT is illogical if it doesn't support its conclusion.

MAMMAL A type of animal that suckles its young (that feeds its young using its breasts or mammary glands).

MOLECULE A tiny, invisible particle made out of ATOMS. Physical matter is made out of MOLECULES.

NEURON One of the tiny cells out of which our brains and nervous systems are made.

A NEURON

PARANORMAL Beyond the normal. For example, some believe that we have a sixth sense called ESP in addition to our normal five senses of sight, taste, touch, hearing and smell.

PHILOSOPHY The question: What is philosophy? is itself a philosophical question. Philosophers disagree over what philosophy is, exactly. In this book I have tried to give you a feel for what philosophy is by giving you examples of the kind of questions philosophers struggle with.

PHYSICAL WORLD/UNIVERSE/MATTER PHYSICAL MATTER is made out of ATOMS and MOLECULES. The physical universe is the universe we seem able to observe around us with our five senses. The only matter in the physical universe is PHYSICAL MATTER.

PSEUDO-SCIENCE Something that *seems* like science, but isn't.

RATIONAL Supported by REASON and good ARGUMENT. JUSTIFIED.

REASON You and I can both REASON: we can think and work things out. We also talk about having a reason to believe something. A reason to believe is something that supports a belief, that makes the belief *more likely* to be true.

201

SCIENCE System of knowledge arrived at by means of observation and experiment.

SOUL A SUPERNATURAL object made out of non-PHYSICAL MATTER: 'soul stuff'. A soul is capable of existing on its own quite independently of anything in the PHYSICAL UNIVERSE. According to those who believe in the existence of souls, it is your soul that thinks, feels, is conscious, has experiences, makes decisions, and so on.

SUPERNATURAL Not part of the natural, PHYSICAL UNIVERSE governed by the LAWS OF NATURE.

Also by Stephen Law

the Philosophy Files

Contains some of the most mind-blowing thoughts ever
thought!

* **How do you know your parents aren't virtual?**
* **Why does the universe exist?**
* **Could you become a robot?**
* **Is there a God?**

Dip in and be amazed at philosophical puzzles as old as the hills
and as topical as today!

"Accessible, entertaining, the only question it doesn't tackle
head on is why nobody's written a book like it before... It's
philosophy in action rather than philosophy in aspic."

The Guardian

"Superb" Amazon.co.uk

"Stephen Law has the happy knack of being able to cut a
complicated question... down to its essentials, and dress it up in
an entertaining, yet enlightening way. Although aimed at
children, it's actually the best introduction to philosophy that
I've read for ages."

Tim LeBon in *Practical Philosophy*

"This is an outstanding introduction to philosophy. Stephen Law
is an exceptionally talented writer. He manages to communicate
the basics of philosophy in an entertaining and accessible style.
I'm envious of his ability."

Nigel Warburton, Philosopher